BMW R75.

Escaping from the Falaise-Pocket:

From Photo to Model; the Complete Story.

By Robert Doepp

INTRODUCTION

Motorcycles have been a passion of mine since early adulthood. When I had to give up riding and came back to modelling, more heavily armoured machines became the focus of my interest and so I never found a link between these two hobbies of mine.
Everything changed when I came over the inspiring picture in Jean Paul Pallud's great book on the German retreat from Normandy which would finally become the base for the ambitious project I am about to describe in this book. It shows four German Paratroopers of an unknown unit trying to escape from the Falaise pocket on a BMW R75 in late August of 1944. It was taken by a soldier of the "Propagandakompanie 698" named "Casper" in the village of Bourgthéroulde.

But there were several steps to take in-between.
When Tasca brought out their 1:24 scale Zündapp KS750 it became my first attempt to build a scale model motorcycle. I integrated it into a little scene depicting the Falaise theme with three self-sculpted figures (a detailed four-part description of this project has been published in AFV-Modeller issues 73-76).

Left above Me at the age of about 26 on my custom-built Harley-Davidson Panhead chopper.
Left Me nowadays at about double the age with the restored BMW R75 (unfortunately not mine!)

In fact, this project had at first been planned as a test run for rebuilding the initial scene in 1:24 scale whenever Tasca would release a BMW R75 kit (which as far as I know was the company's original plan). But firstly, this never happened, and secondly I really got fascinated by the Zündapp and so I decided to do another one in 1:9 scale. I relied on the outdated ESCI/Revell kit from the late 1970s which required a complete makeover to reach the level of detail I was after. I had already collected some experience in scratch-building and sculpting in the larger scales with my 1:10 "Roll Over Beethoven" project (a detailed two-part description was published in AFV-Modeller issues 82-83) and so I went rather courageously into what turned out to be a heavily time consuming project requiring a fair amount of research and detail work.

Tasca's 1:24
Zündapp KS750

Due to these former experiences I was clearly aware of several characteristics which would also determine my current project :
- Virtually nothing on a motorcycle model is hidden from the viewer's eye. Some planning and extra effort is necessary not only to rebuild the detail but also to pre-paint and weather numerous sub-assemblies.
- The famous German war motorcycles, BMW R75 and Zündapp KS750 in particular, are still driven, repaired and traded by enthusiasts worldwide, therefore one can rely on repair manuals, parts lists and internet displays selling parts or complete motorcycles which provide references the average tank-modeller can only dream of.
- The large scale offers the opportunity to adapt details which are irrelevant or impossible to create in minor scales. This might be called the fun part on the one hand, but on the other it makes any step pretty time-consuming and so some stamina is necessary to finish any larger project.
- Figures made from Magic Sculpt (putty) are really heavy. This of course becomes more virulent in the larger scale when placing them on a delicate model made of plastic.

Despite my previous experiences this project was an adventure rather than a routine and so I would like to invite you to follow me through the many varying steps to take in order to finish an ambitious project like this, which in the end took me about 4,500 hours of modelling time. Personally I feel that one of the circles in my life has come to a pretty satisfying cohesion with it - not at least inspiring me to buy a motorcycle again.
Before I start the detailed description of my BMW R75-based project it is necessary to mention two aspects, that characterized this project in particular but may also be of interest in many other modelling projects:

Scratch-Building
In a modeller's perfect world - well, if there is no perfect model-kit at least, the perfect reference material includes scale drawings and measurements for just about every detail. But we do not live in the perfect modeller's world and despite the masses of material I could rely on, unfortunately I could get my hands only on very few scale drawings or measurements, thus developing dimensions from scaled down photographs was a big part of the process and I will explain the techniques I used in detail.

Rebuilding a Photo
I have made use of war-time pictures many times before as inspiration for some projects or to recreate special aspects. But even if I tried to get close to the real thing, I always claimed for a high degree of artificial licence and kept in mind that a scale model has its own artistically defined standards apart from the ideal of shrunken historical reality.
The latter surely stays true in this special case as well, but nevertheless I started with the ambition to get as close to the original photo as possible. Unfortunately my ambition reached its limits with many aspects and in many different ways, to describe these will be a necessary part of this book.
A frequent problem was the fact that the photo was taken with a wide-angle lens from a close distance, which caused distortion complicating my estimates of the proportions of the differing elements and taking a similar picture of the model completed. Another rather striking example occurred with the rubber tyres. This particular BMW R75 shows a slightly bigger tyre on the front wheel, which I identified as being of "Kübelwagen" type. The uppermost of the total of four spare wheels seems to be similar. Unfortunately the available Revell kit "Kübelwagen" tyres proved to be far too big.

Scratchbuilt 1:10 “Roll over Beethoven”

1:9 ESCI / Revell
Zündapp KS750

1

I decided to use custom-made items for these two wheels. They were produced by the German Pistor company following my guidelines, but they did not get as close to their paragon as I had hoped for.
In addition I never found out of what type the three other spare wheels were. So I decided to use the Revell BMW kit tires for these even though they do not perfectly match the photo.
Dealing with these kind of failures is part of my ambition to really tell the complete story of this project. The same is true for the additional chapters accompanying the description of making the model itself; some original war-time pictures of the BMW R75 and also some detail-shots of a restored vehicle.
Hopefully this will allow you to take a look behind the often secretly kept process of making an ambitious long-term project like this. I hope you may benefit from this approach even if the BMW R75 - as a rather involved subject for some modellers I suppose, is not in the heart of your usual modelling interests.

Along with the Zündapp KS750, the BMW R75 was the very first German motorcycle originally designed for military use. In particular both motorcycles had a differential which drove the sidecar wheel providing superb cross country performance, and the first hydraulic foot brake, which affected the rear and sidecar wheel at the same time. These features were what made their riding characteristics, both types where never in war-time use as solo-machines.

Basically designed in 1937/38 the BMW R75 reached its first serial production stage in early 1941 and it was from that point delivered to the German troops in growing numbers until in October 1944 a heavy air raid on Eisenach, to where the production had been transferred to from Munich in mid 1942, stopped the production run after about 16,500 units.
Its original purpose was to be used for reconnaissance missions in the "Kradschützen" units (motorcycle battalions). These were lacking both armour and heavy weaponry, and so their missions started to cause unbearable losses. Therefore the BMW's main duties changed to multi-purpose use in varying units, in the "Fallschirmjäger" (paratrooper) battle groups it was still in use throughout the war as a light-weight fighting vehicle, which even could be para-dropped in a special protecting cage or transported in a Ju-52 aircraft.

The BMW R75 in the picture I have chosen shows several features of a late war model. It has the late type air cleaner cover placed on top of the fuel tank (introduced in mid 1942), the late type protective rubber gaiters on the front fork (introduced in May 1943) along with the late type flat, large diameter front fender and late type tongue-secured mounts for the sheet metal stowage boxes.
Unfortunately it shows a front licence plate as well, which had officially been dropped before some of the visible late type features were introduced.
Nevertheless I decided to depict a late production model and chose the serial number 765 412 produced in October 1943 - with a front licence plate as field unit modification (for numerous changes in production in relation to serial numbers see Hommes 2009, pages 8-10 in particular).

Another strange feature of the chosen subject are the driver´s fabric hand cuffs, which likely were part of the contemporary serial produced hand heating system but the hot-fume ducts for the system itself are obviously not in place.

2

3

Though I was aware that the result would reveal all the mistakes and shortcomings, it was the logical last step to see how close I had managed to come to the original photo. I removed the main subject from the original image with the help of Photoshop and placed the model in front of the resulting background **(1, opposite page)**. To simply lower the colour saturation was a first step to virtually enhance the realistic impression **(2)** followed by completely converting the picture into black and white mode **(3)** and finally hiding the base **(4, below)** - everything done with Photoshop software.

4

BMW

1

CONSTRUCTION

WHEELS AND FRAME

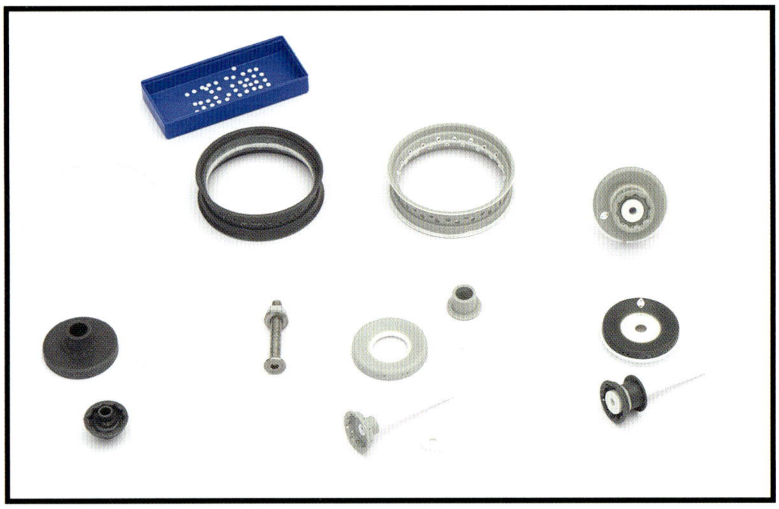

The spokes are cut off and their positions are marked by small holes (dark grey plastic parts). The 4mm screw was used to fix the brake drums into a handyman drill. The pecking is represented by punched plastic tiles, which needed to be drilled extremely carefully after gluing with several drills of increasing diameter (middle parts). On the right you see the completed hub (dark grey version disassembled), which was kept traversable to the drum brake until the spokes were fitted. As I needed a total of seven wheels I had to buy at least two kits, that's why the plastic colour shows two tones of grey. In fact I used three kits in total for the project but only two are necessary.

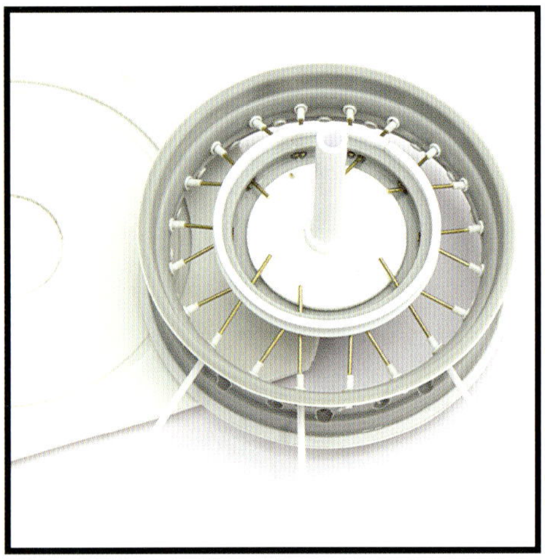

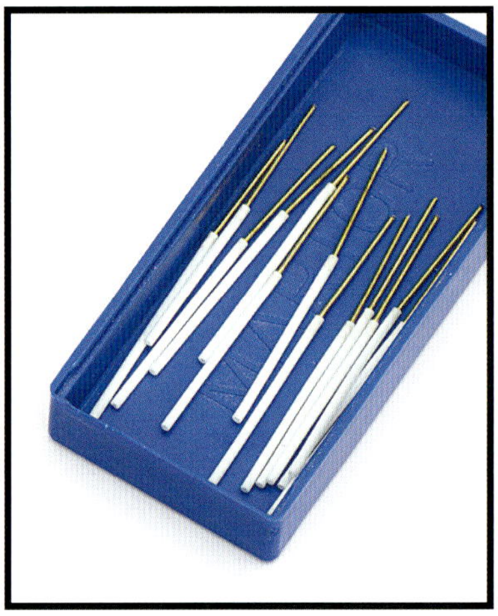

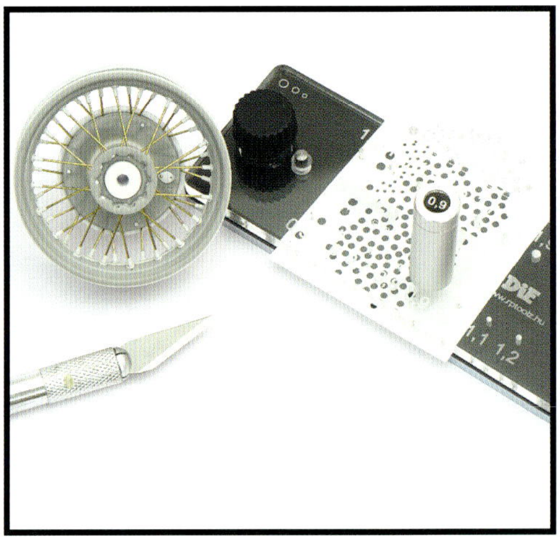

I started construction with the wheels. These were standard items with BMW R75 and Zündapp KS750 and so I felt already familiar with this task.
All three main wheels were identical and showed the same concave shaped drum brake. Unfortunately with the kit it is represented as a plain version. As the right side spokes are fixed to the brake drum, the dimensions of the parts completely changed when I cut the brake drums and carefully hollowed them while turning in the usual 'handyman' drill with adjustable rpm-range set at the lowest possible rpm. At the same time the kit's brake drums were way too thin. I thickened them with u-shaped plastic material to a correct width and approximately recreated the kit part outer diameter.

It had proved impossible to exactly preserve the ratio between drum brake, wheel hub and the two lines of spokes. I firstly only fixed the split parts by gluing a plastic shim to the hub from behind so that it could still be traversed in place later on.

The kit tires were massively cast and showed a thick inner lip fixing them firmly to the rim while gluing the latter along with the hub and brake drum. As I wanted to glue the rim separately I had to cut the inner parts of the tires with a hobby knife so they could be pushed onto the finished wheel after assembly. In order to enhance their fit I had to slightly thicken the rims outer lips.

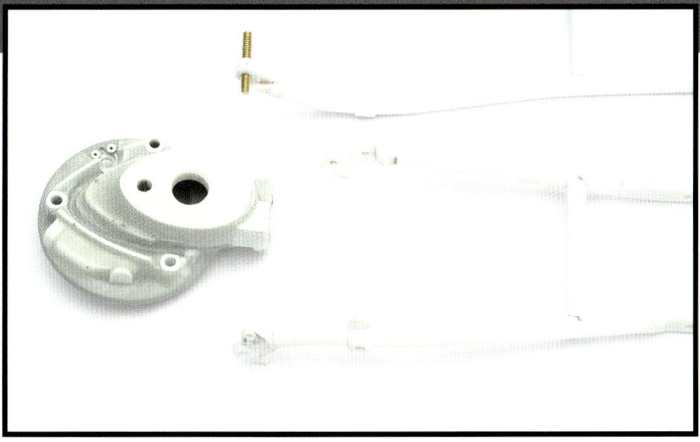

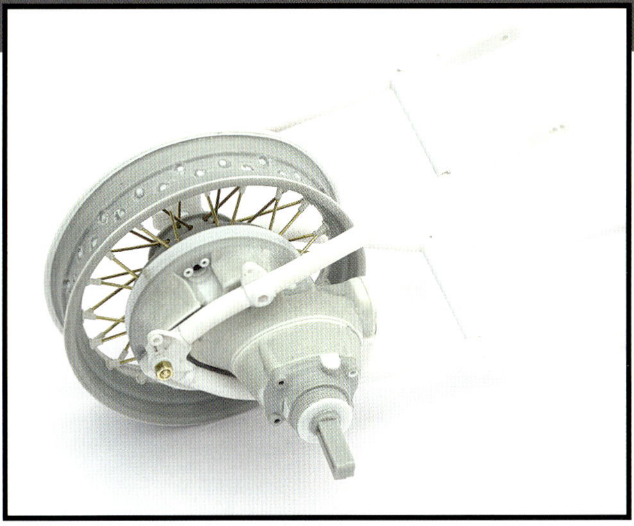

All model frame tubes were constructed of plastic tubing with thick copper wire fitted inside which strengthened them and allowed curving without any heat treatment or distortion.

The only ratio which was preserved throughout all these changes (and I was at the same time sure about due to reference drawings) was the one between the outer side of the hub and the outer rim. I made a simple jig from plastic card to provisionally fix this side's spoke ratio and started to add the spoke replacements made of brass wire and drilled plastic rod. As the inner side was completed the hub could be traversed into position and fixed with the outer side's spokes. While I carefully cut the brass end of the spokes to length beforehand, the plastic end was kept overlength and cut after gluing. Though the brass end was only fixed with small punched plastic tiles the brass spokes provided superb strength to the finished wheels.

Unlike the Zündapp, the BMW showed a rather complexly shaped multi-part frame with an asymmetrical back end obviously constructed tightly around the differential as one of the determining characteristics of the motorcycle.

I also started the model's construction with the differential. Its outer shape was identical to that of the Zündapp so I had already a clear idea of the necessary changes. While I cut the kit part into the same sub units as the original item I strengthened the parts with an internal thick plastic rod as this would become one of the main connecting points between the motorcycle and the sidecar frame.

Fortunately I found high resolution pictures of a disassembled replica frame on the 'net which made it possible to measure it's size ratios from the back end as a starting point. I adapted the back end to the differential and rear wheel at first. When I had rebuilt the original sheet metal pressed "Sattelstütze" (saddle support) the back end reached the necessary strength to adapt and fix the bare rear fender.

Because the split front-end's lower section was fixed by a shaft reaching through the front engine mount I had to construct both items parallel in order to strengthen the construction and make sure of an exact fit.

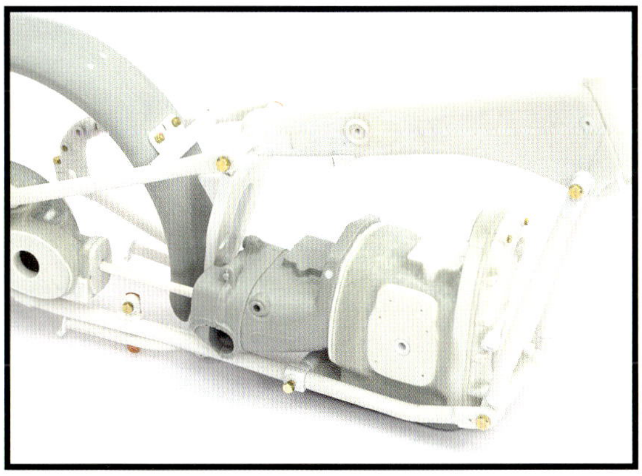

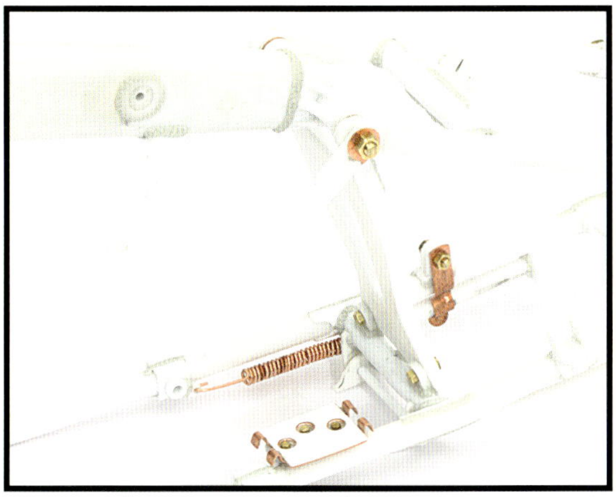

The engine originally was not placed exactly in the middle of the frame. The right side of the front mount showed a bushing. The back mount was fixed along with the foot rests. Differing bushings at both sides adapted the engine to the frame at the back mount also.

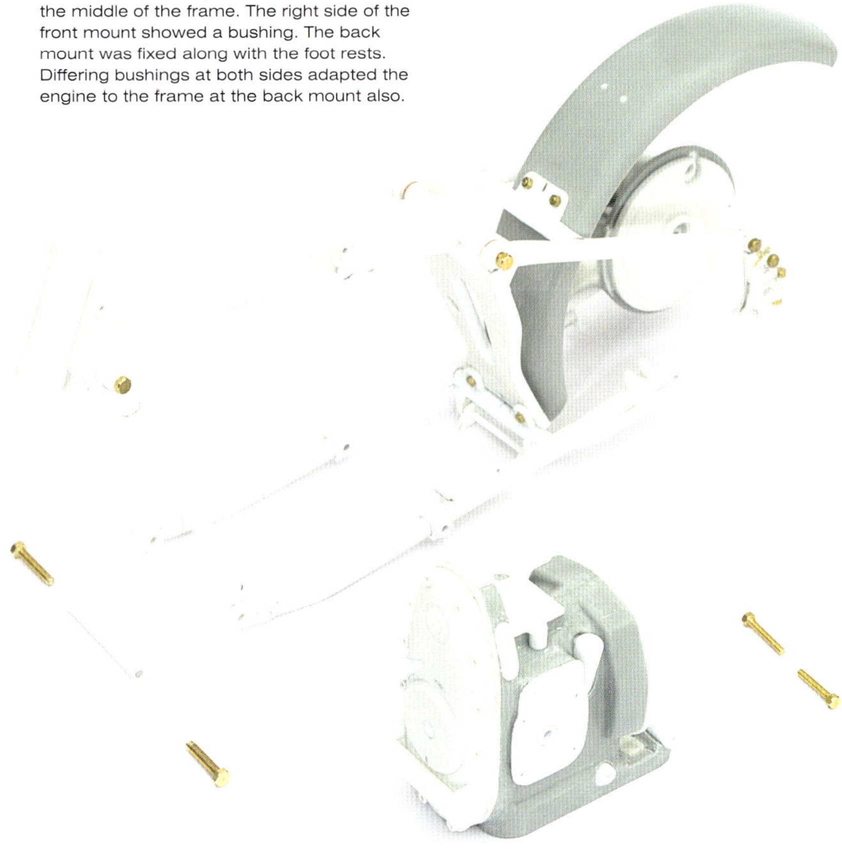

TRANSMISSION

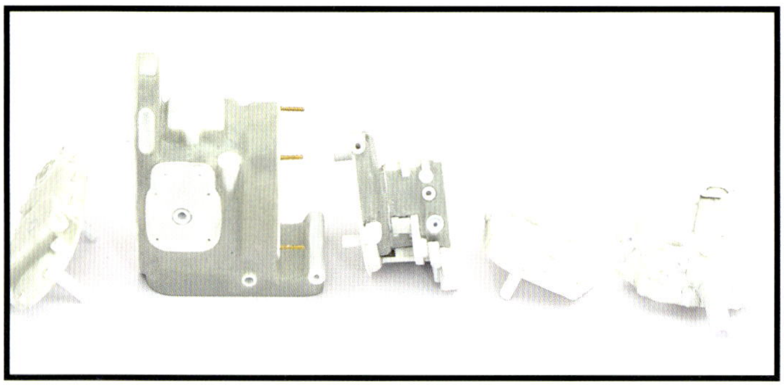

The picture shows the different stages of construction: Timing cover and crankcase are already smoothed and detailed with Magic Sculp while the three sections of the transmission are only roughly constructed with plastic parts (partly taken from the kit).

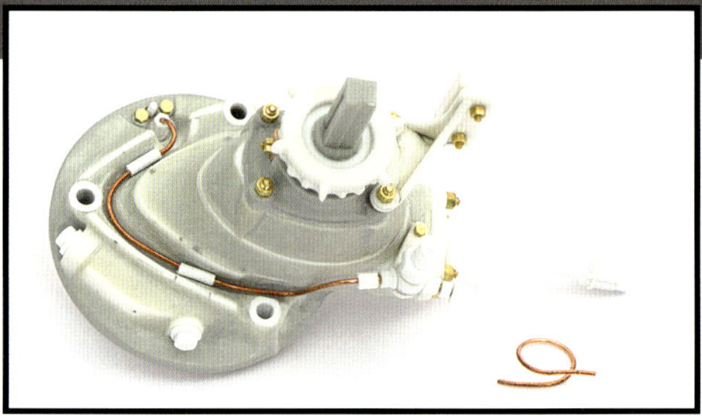

The cardan-shaft is already detailed and fitted to the differential. The differential originally split the engine power in a 70% - 30% ratio between rear and side car wheel to provide straight direction drive. It could be blocked with a lever for driving through rough terrain with maximum power at both wheels.

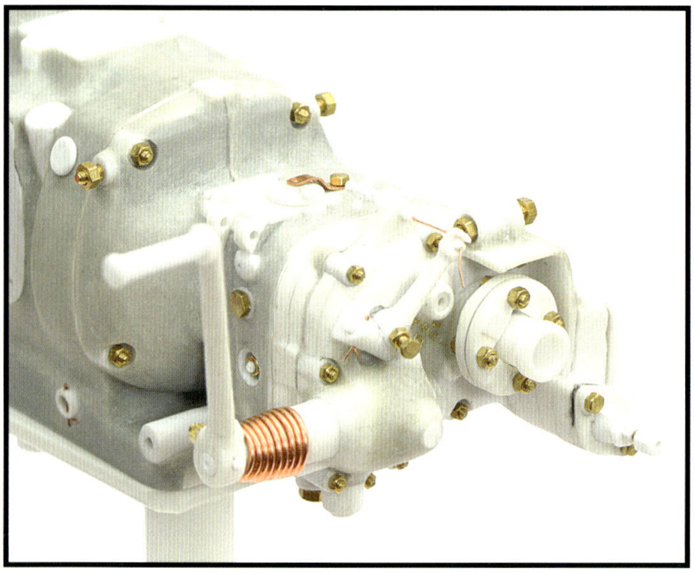

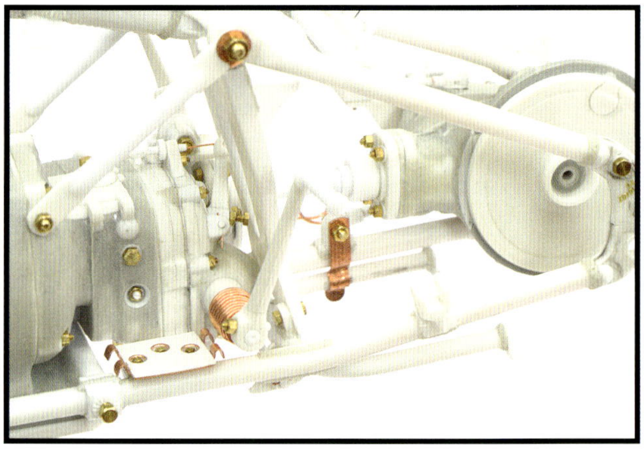

The main stand was fixed with a sheet metal spring, which was screwed to the initial production right pillion foot rest mount. Even though the original use was obsolete when the foot rest itself was mounted to the differential later on the mount stayed in place to hold the spring. Notice how the clutch lever reaches through a hole in the saddle support: A true challenge for model construction!

The transmission, originally bolted to the back of the crankcase, is one of the poorest kit parts. It only served as a starting point but it's back end had to be completely replaced but it was necessary to set its basic shape at this particular stage because its upper mount had to be connected to the top joint between the back and the front-frame section strengthening both these main components. After these steps I was sure about the fitting of all components and so could finally refine all of them separately. Starting with the basic frame I then went onto to the transmission and the differential along with the foot brake system.

Work on the frame was finally finished when I had added the driver's foot rests and the left side protective tubing for the cylinder because these items were screwed to the main joints of the frame and also the engine.

Whenever possible I made use of brass screws and nuts in order to connect the sub-assemblies because I was not totally sure which of them I would need to remove in order to keep them 'paintable'. The multi-part construction of the frame made it possible to push this technique to the limits - though it interfered with my aim to strengthen the whole construction as a base for the predictably heavy figures.

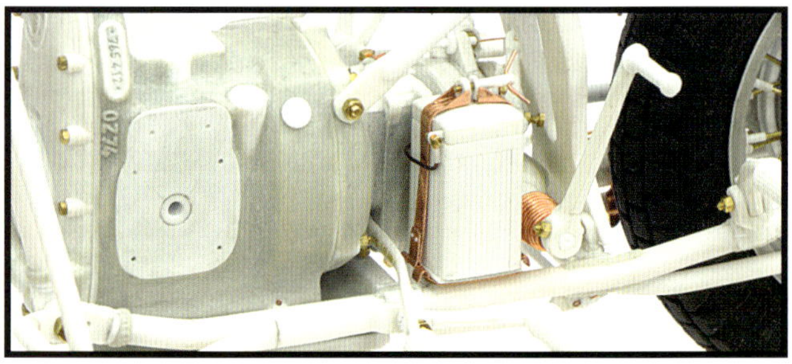

The battery rested on a small sheet metal plate screwed to the frame. The identification "OZ74" on the engine marked it being capable for low quality fuel of the "OktanZahl" (octane number) 74. This was necessary for the use of coal-generated fuel and therefore a standard item on many German vehicles.

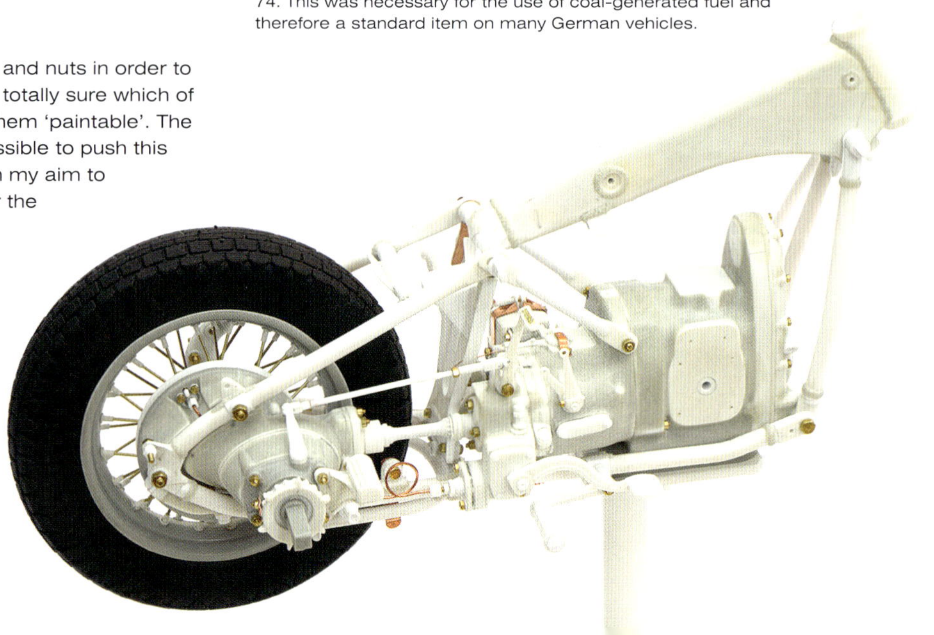

REAR FENDER

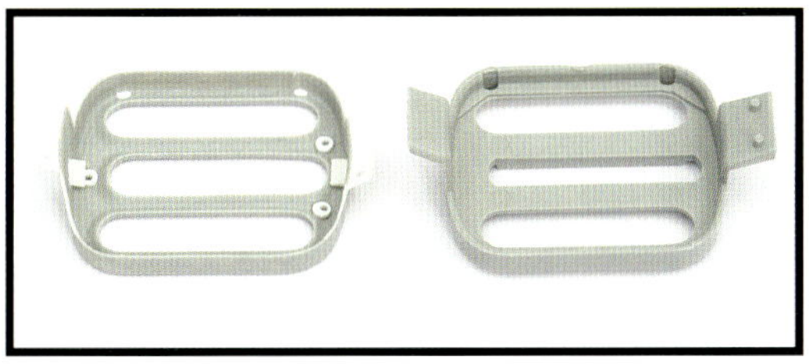

The reworked pillion base part on the left. Similar to the original I cut inner threads to added 'punched' styrene that would later on allow me to fix the pillion seat.

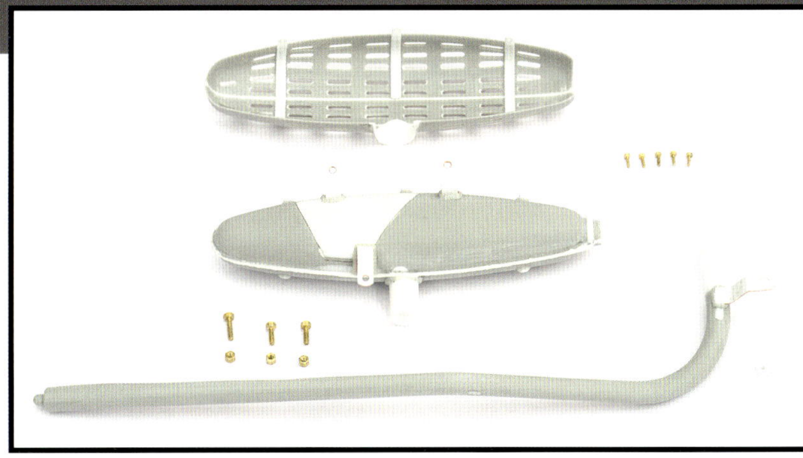

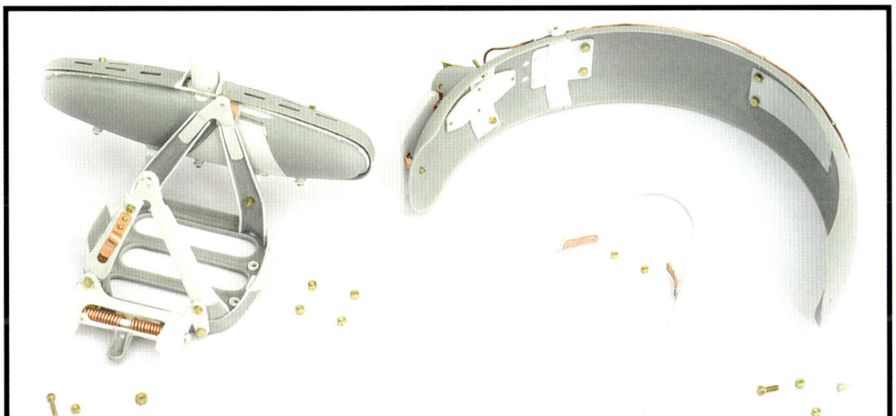

The picture gives an idea of all underside details. These components were removable at first but in the end I chose not to remove the rear fender, support and carrier base from the frame for the painting process.

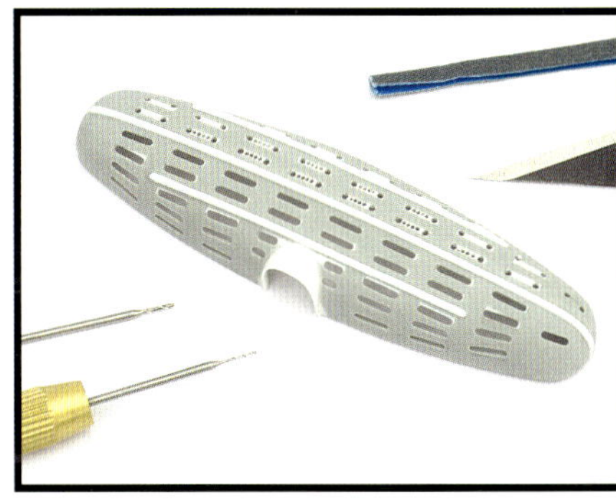

With the origina,l the main exhaust pipe was only fixed with a single butterfly nut along with the rear fender support tube. In the end I glued it to the muffler instead but kept the heat shield separate and the muffler removable from the carrier struts.

Though I had already basically adapted the rear fender in the frame construction, adding all of the components fixed to it proved a true challenge mainly because of the asymmetrical character of the frame. I started with base carrier top part, whose kit representation had to be thinned, detailed and fixed to the prepared fender. Once the struts had been glued to the carrier and screw fixed to the frame, I did similar with the supporting bracket, both following the asymmetrical layout of the frame's back end.

One more prominent detail was the sheet metal stowage box, which I decided to finish along with its two counterparts fixed to the sidecar body. On the right side the rear muffler was to be added including it's typical heat shield.

Again all main components were not glued but screw fixed as it would otherwise have been impossible to disassemble them for painting.

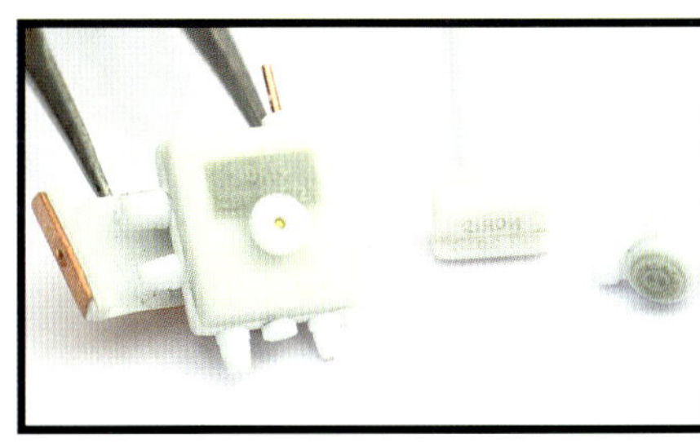

The fuse box was screwed to the saddle support. Marked "Noris" this was sculpted mirrored into a plastic stamp in order to make a raised version from Magic Sculp. I did the same with the "BMW" logo on the plug.

The cover locks were basically cut from 0.25mm sheet styrene. They all were workable until I glued them to the boxes.

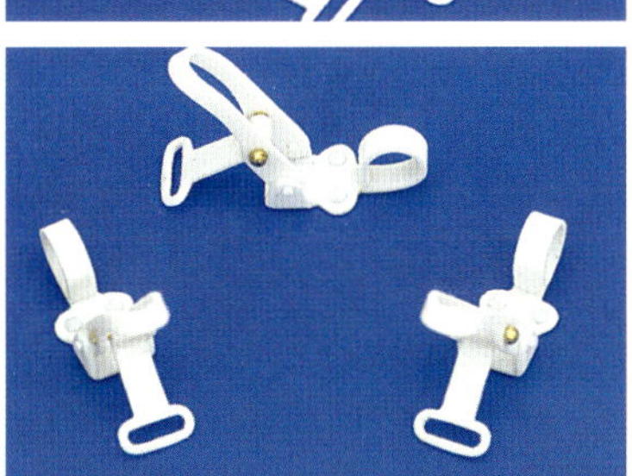

The handles were made of drilled plastic rod and copper wire. The frames were made of standard Evergreen parts.

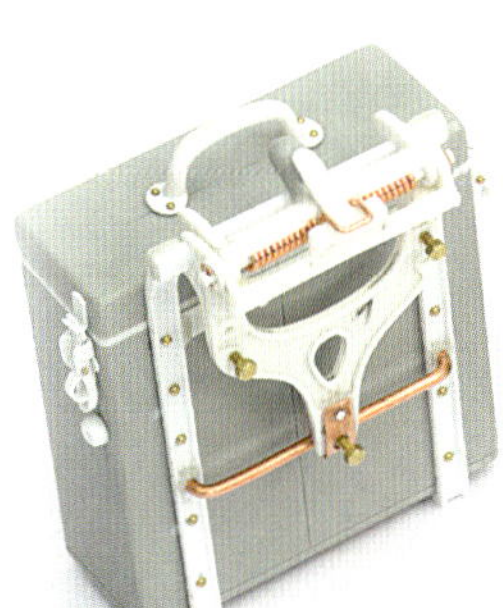

A cast doubled hook mechanism covered a twisted spring to fix the stowage boxes to their mounting brackets. I started to rebuild this mechanism from a rough version rotating on a drill.

The late style hook mechanism showed an additional securing tongue. Everything had to be made in a workable condition in order to allow the stowage boxes to be removed and painted separately.

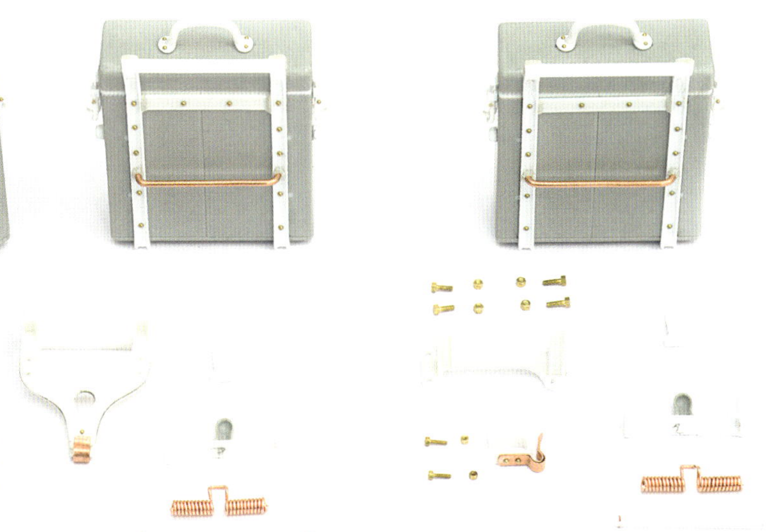

SEATS

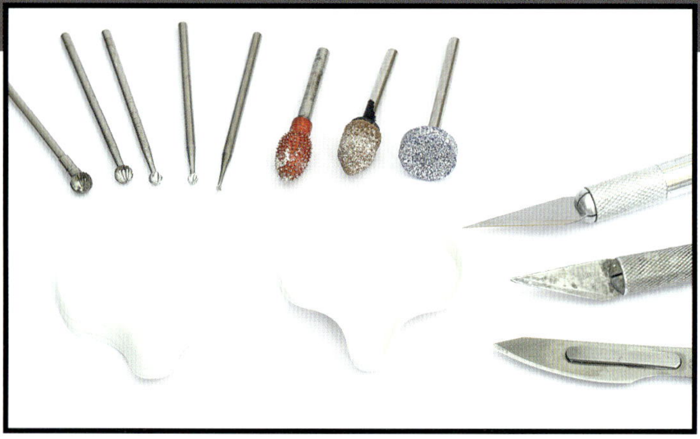

The drill bits were used with a flexible shaft fitted to a handyman drill with adjustable rpm-range. The surface had to be smoothened afterwards with various blades - and lots of sanding.

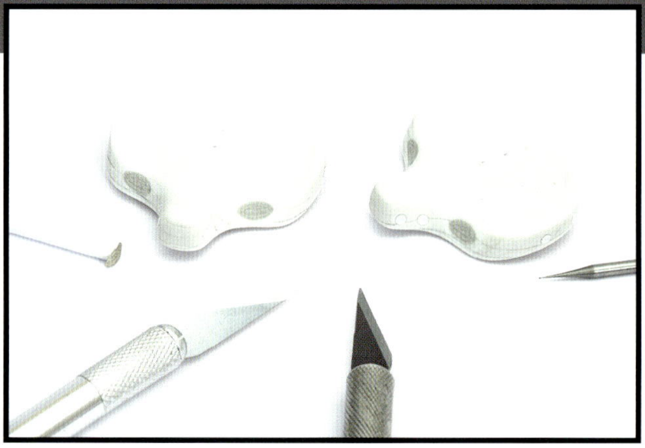

The inner seat surfaces were structured with a 0.3mm ball shaped drill bit. The "Drilastic"trademark was created with the help of an ABER PE-stamp (Z-P176) pressed into Magic Sculp shape.

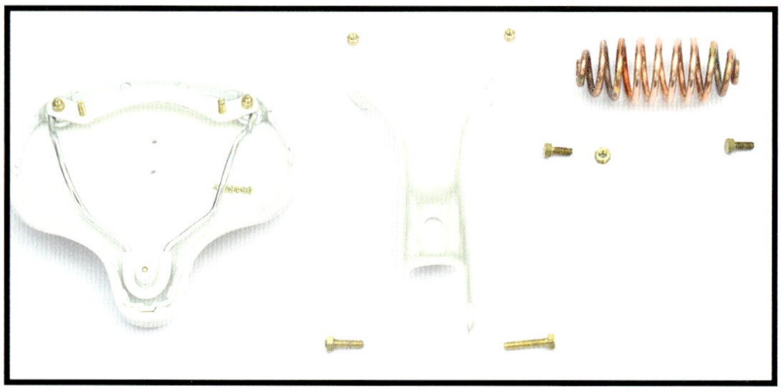

Though the springing system is rather simple it was pretty tricky to make the originally pressed sheet metal-made base part from 0.7mm plastic card, which I glued, sanded and smoothened with Magic Sculp. The spring ends were heat treated to allow closer bending.

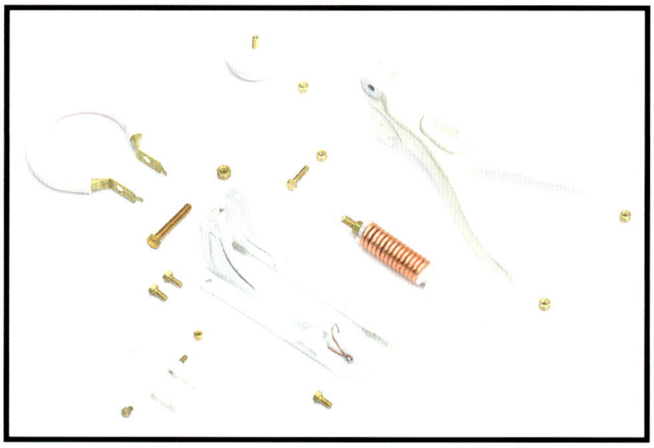

The spring system could be fixed in three different positions (three holes in the seats main support) to adapt the pillion's weight. While not in use it had to be locked into a slightly upward position by the small lock on the left reaching into the hook at the support's lower front end to keep it from damage.

Because it's mount is hidden underneath the fuel tank at least the driver's seat had to be finished beforehand. Both seats were basically identical while their mountings differed. As the kit provides the seats in a soft black material, impossible to rework, these had to be replaced by items glued from several layers of plastic card, which I shaped with a variety of tools. In order to compensate the rigid frame both seats were outfitted with a springing system. It took me quite some research work to reconstruct these items, in most images hardly visible!

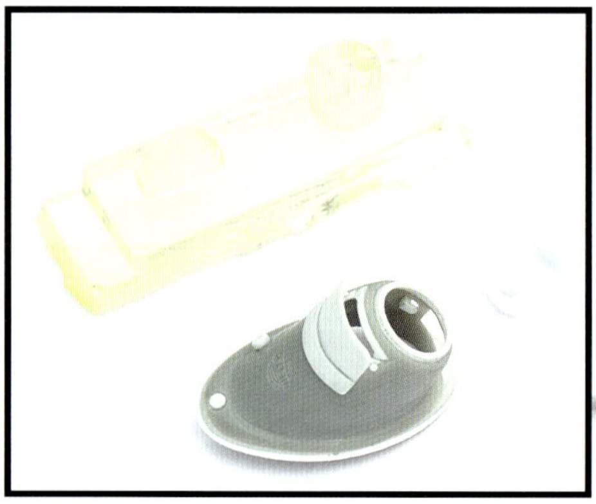

The glass parts were first made of styrene and cast from clear resin afterwards. Notice the "Hella" factory-logo sculpted into the backlight body with the tip of a hobby knife.

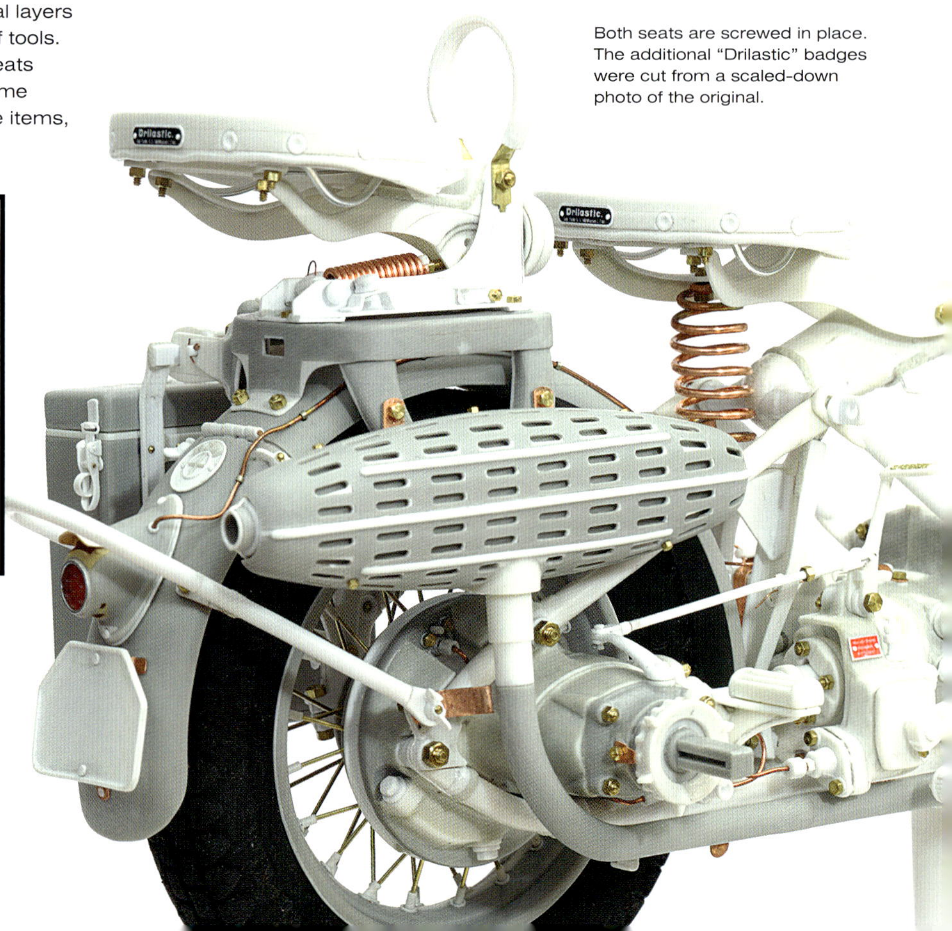

Both seats are screwed in place. The additional "Drilastic" badges were cut from a scaled-down photo of the original.

FUEL TANK

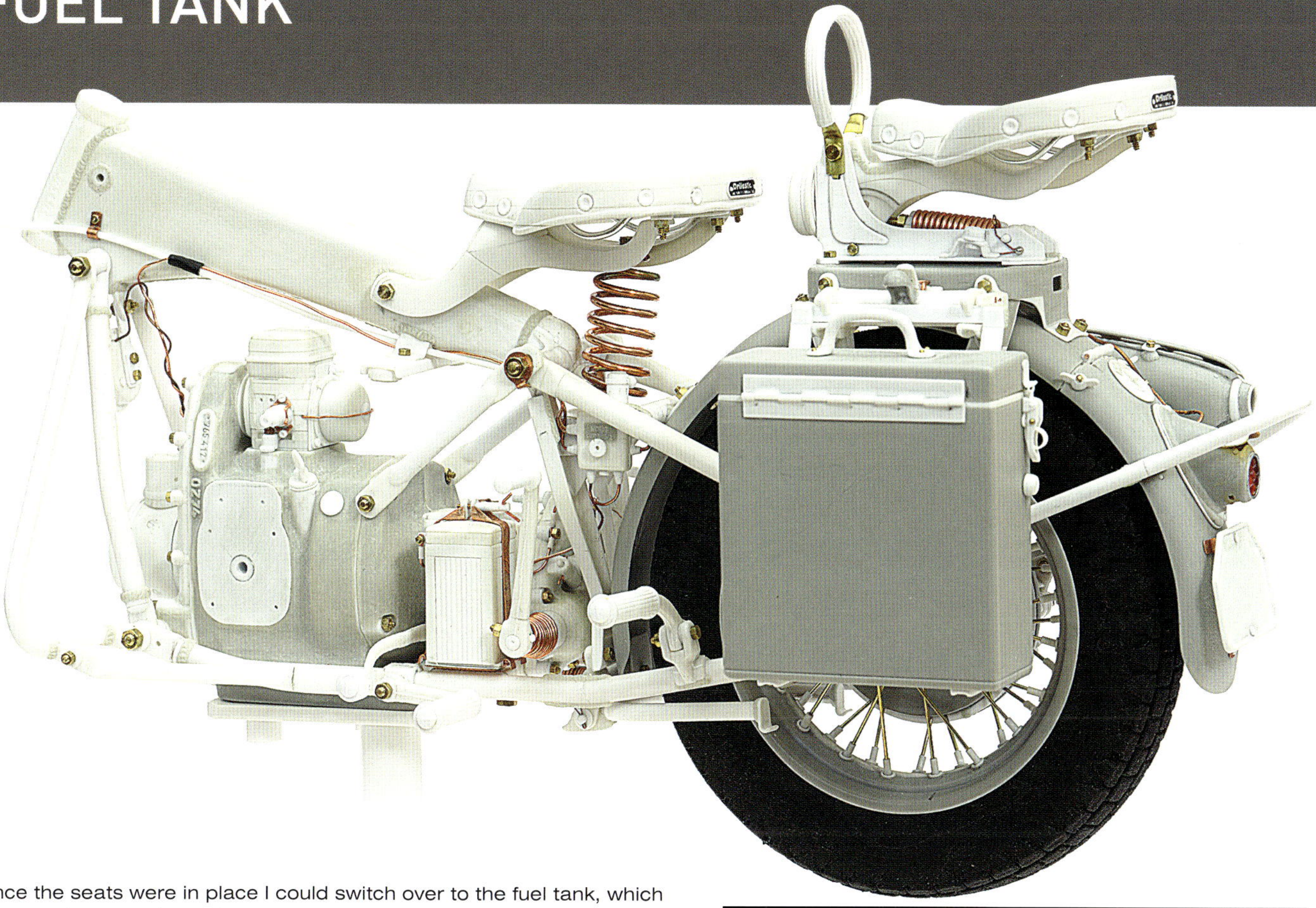

Once the seats were in place I could switch over to the fuel tank, which was a rather complex unit as not only the hand shifting system was fixed to it but, with the late war BMW R75 model, the air cleaning system as well. Before it could be placed some additional details had to be added to the areas hard to reach afterwards; the magneto ignition system on top of the crankcase, the horn and the generator/regulator-unit including all necessary electrical wiring.

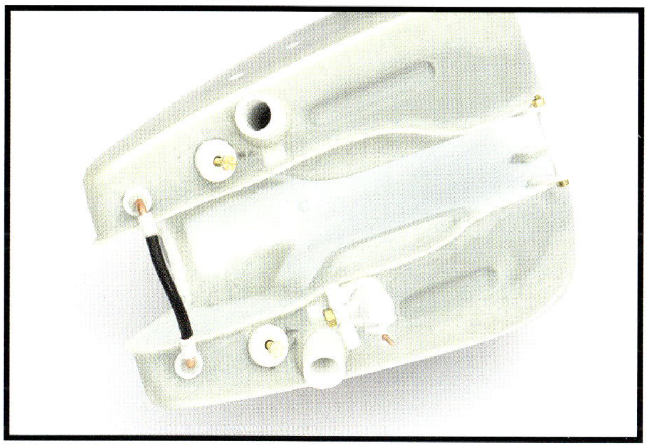

Beside the lack of detail the kit part was way too round-ish. I glued some plastic card in order to reshape the edges and again smoothened everything with Magic Sculp.

Starting in mid 1942 the air cleaner was no longer placed on the transmission housing but a larger version on top of gas tank. The air supply feed for both carburetors led through the gas tank fitting tightly between fixing-points, gas tap and hand shifting mechanism.

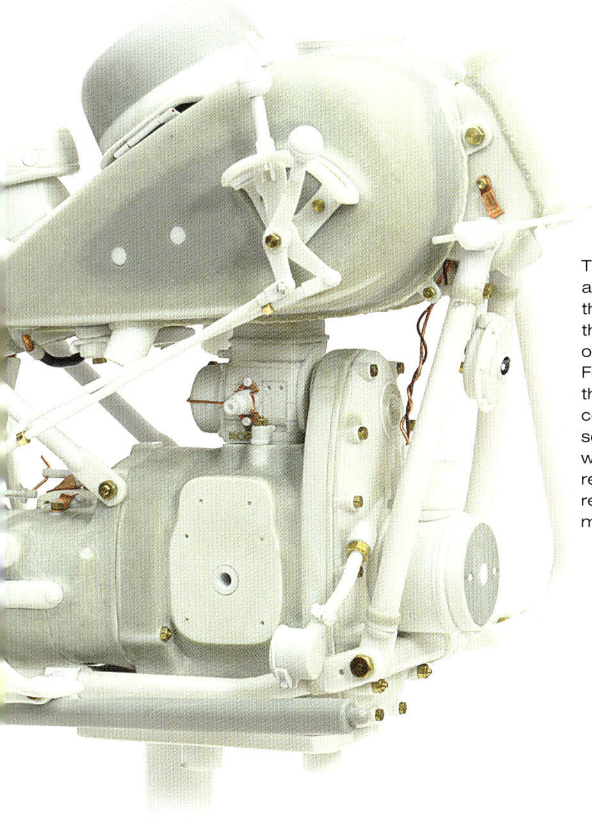

The generator was added to the front of the timing cover and the small regulator on top of it. Fortunately originally these were connected internally so that only the wiring leading to the regulator had to be represented with the model.

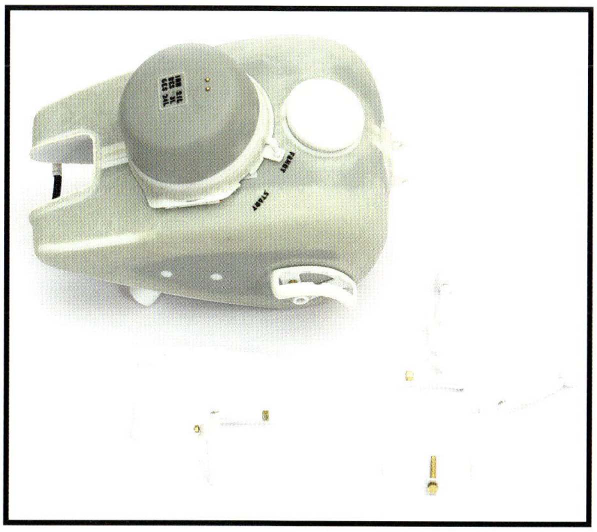

The inner lever shifted the gears "R,1,L,2,3,4", the outer lever allowed to choose between "Gelände" (cross country) and "Strasse" (street) mode. The black marking for filling quantities and choke position ("Fahrt"/Drive) come from the Archer range (AR88007).

ENGINE CYLINDERS

I was aware that making the complete cylinder-units from scratch would be one of the more challenging parts of construction. That maybe made me postpone the procedure to the latest possible point.
A scaled down photo of the crankcase taken from a repair manual gave me the dimensions of the cylinder's base as a proper starting point to which I could adapt also scaled down photos of the cylinders by measuring the cylinder bore.
The following construction of the complexly shaped finned cylinders could be based on approximate measurements. The construction of the even more complexly shaped cylinder heads followed the same technique, because not only the bore but the drilled gasket surfaces as well made it possible to scale down proper photos to exactly the same size. Afterwards the late style rocker covers could be added to finish the whole unit. Screwing the cylinders to the engine case finally allowed me to adapt the front muffler, the carburettors and the spark plugs along with the ignition cables. I had made a handle with thick plastic rods reaching into tubing inside the engine case to allow secure handling.
This had to be finally dropped when it came to create the detail of the engine's underside before the sheet metal knee-shield finished the work on the motorcycle's torso.

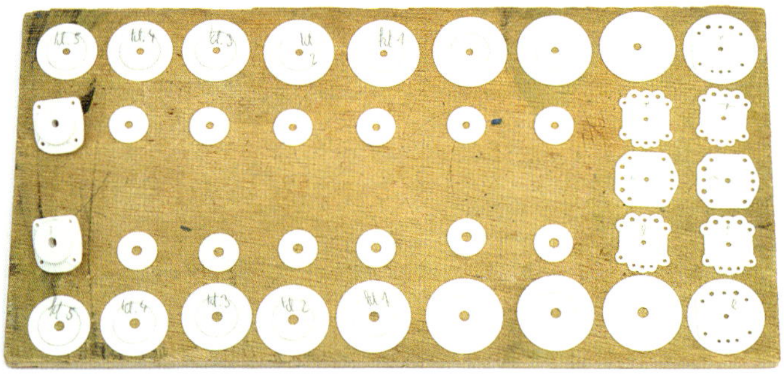

The inner sections were made from 0.5mm plastic card, the outer fins from 0.3mm. The last two inner fins were complexly shaped because they incorporated six threats for the head screws and supports for the tappets (on top) and oil lines (bottom).

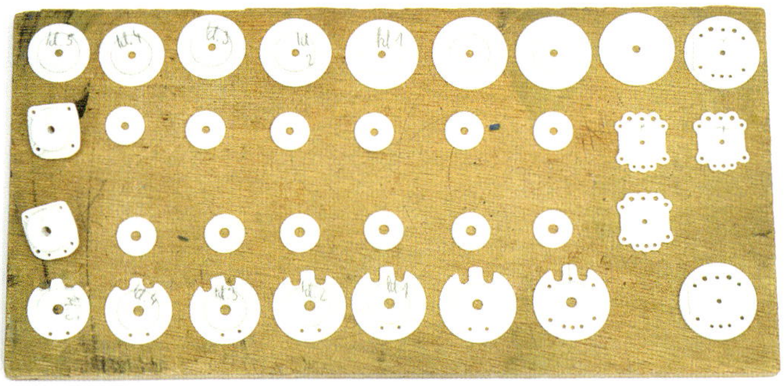

Only the outer fins of the lower cylinder are already drilled for the oil lines and cut for the tappets. The third outer fin was at first adapted to the already glued outer end and used as a stencil for the inner ones. I used different sizes for the centered drilling holes of both cylinders to avoid mixing them up.

The outer gasket surfaces of the cylinders were doubled before gluing them to the last cooling fin. The copies (below in the middle) would serve later on as the corresponding gasket surface of the cylinder head.

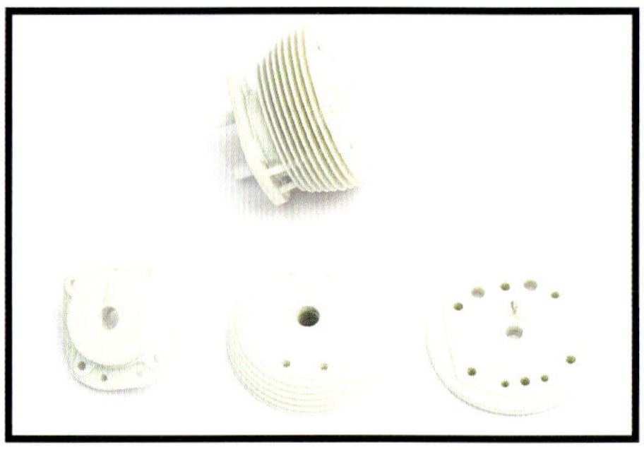

Three sub-units were glued in the end to finish the basic shape. 0.8mm Plastruct-rod represents the oil lines.

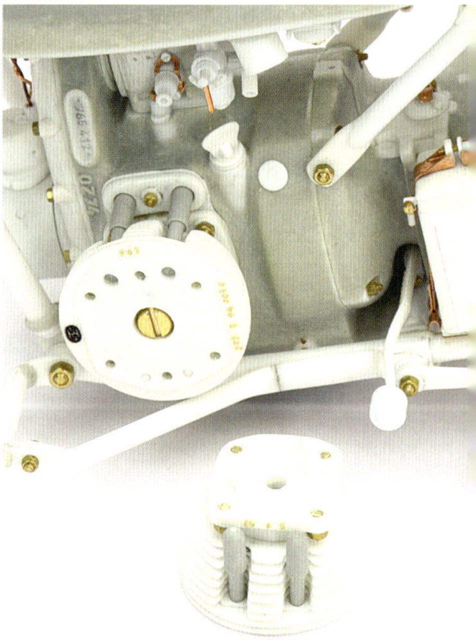

The finished cylinders with all necessary details. The cylinder base nuts are just fake, the model parts are held in place by central slotted screw instead. The cast numbers come from Paper Panzer Productions (PPP 35017).

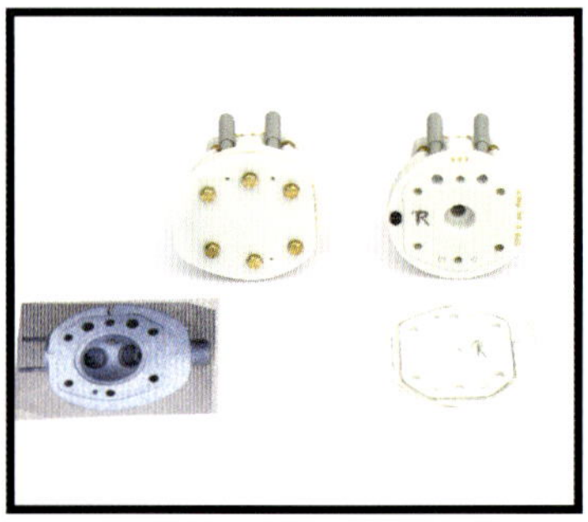

The prepared gasket surface part was used to scale down a photo of the cylinder head and start with the first cooling fin.

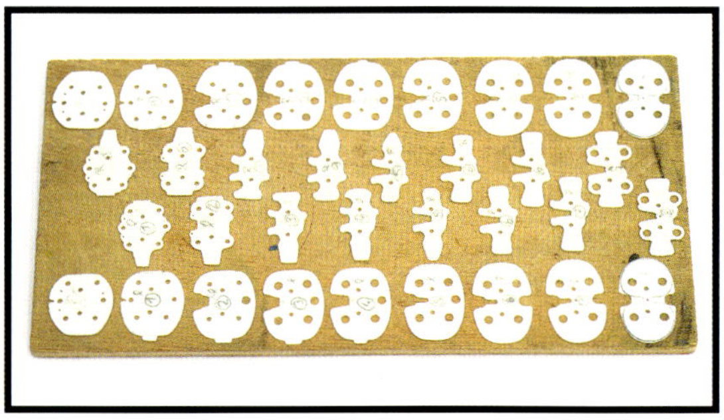

Onto the cylinder heads. The inner structure was made from 0.7mm plastic sheet, the outer fins from 0.3mm, except for the first one which was made of 0.5mm material. The cut-out for the spark plug just between the tappet-casings was what made the job a little tricky.

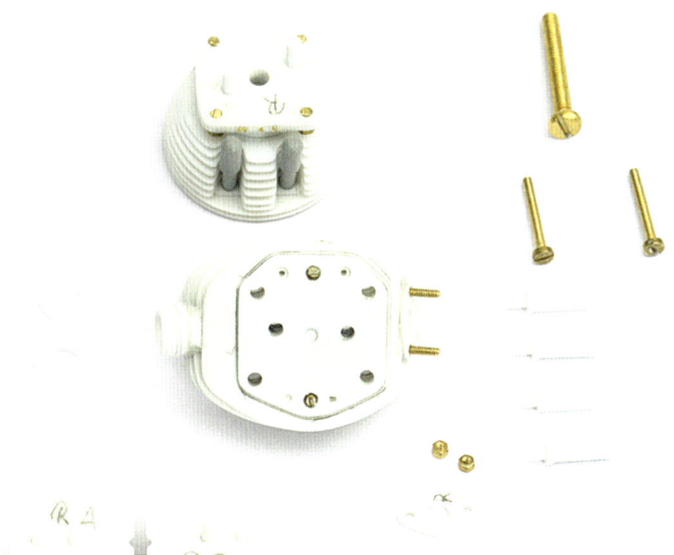

The finished cylinder units. Four head screws on each cylinder had an extended hexagonal head onto which the rockers were mounted. Again all the head screws are fake as on the model two slotted screws hold each head in place instead. Gasket surface parts for the carburettors are already prepared as are the special screw caps for the exhaust pipes.

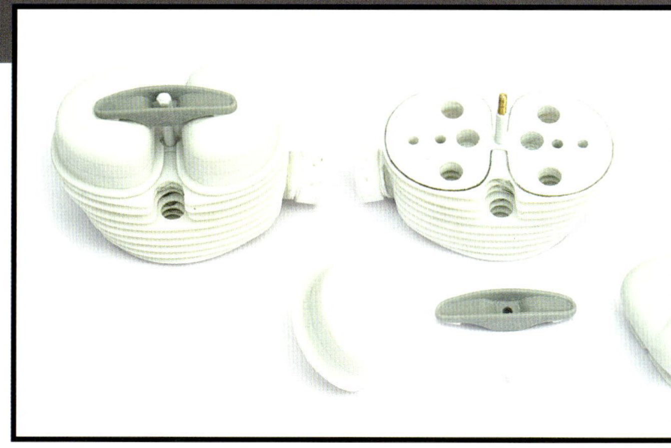

Plastic material was glued to the prepared gasket surfaces of the rocker covers and cut and sanded to shape afterwards. These were held in place by just a single central nut by the help of a cast paw.

The carburettors were based on the model parts but needed some extra detailing and were outfitted with late style heat shields made from 0.1mm copper sheet. The air ducts are not kit parts but were adapted from heat-treated sprue.

A small can filled with fuel, which served for cleaning purposes, was part of the extra equipment. The "Kraftstoff" (fuel) sign was made by the help of a self-made mirrored stamp and Magic Sculp again. I made use of the varying blade tips and sanded needle ends shown to carefully correct the result.
The shield clamps were made of 0.2mm copper sheet and thickened with an additional layer of 0.25mm plastic sheet after bending.

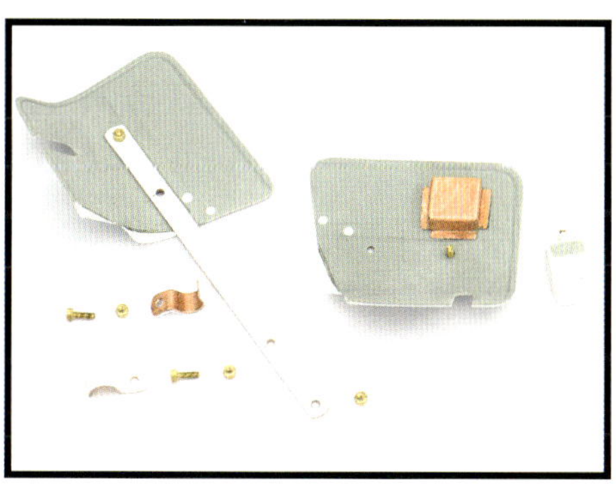

The spark plugs were drilled from Plastruct hexagonal styrene and the parts of the spark plug connector from Plastruct plastic rod. Plastruct parts are slightly harder than their Evergreen counterparts, which makes them better for drilling-purposes.

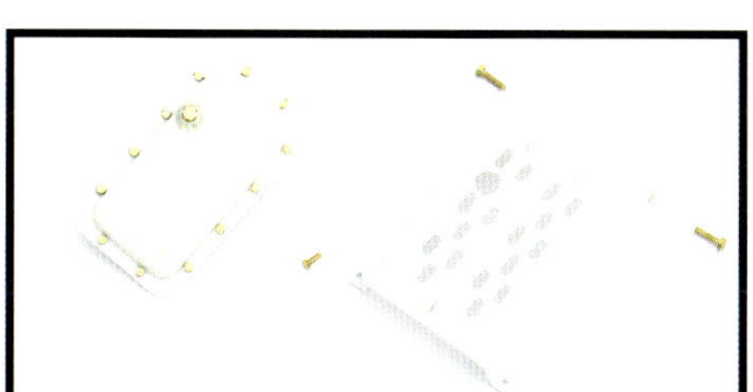

Originally a separate massive protection shield was bolted underneath the engine case to protect the oil sump.

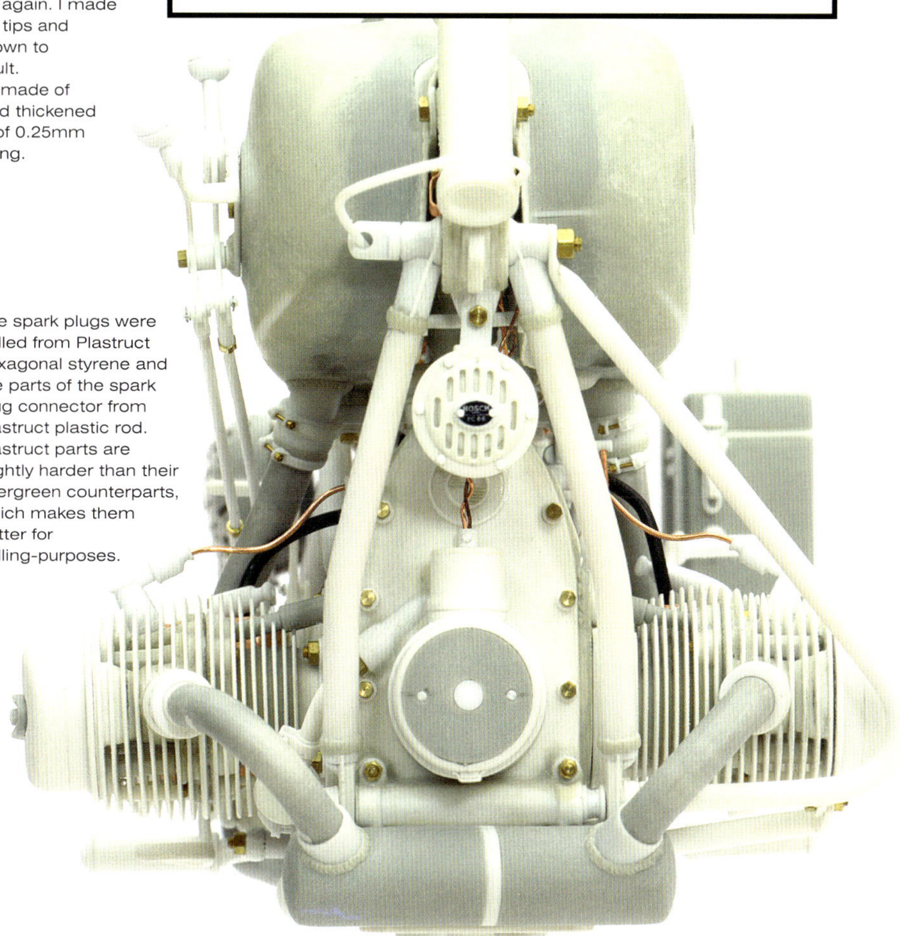

The front muffler ("Sammler") was screwed to the frame along with the engine guard plate. Both front and rear exhaust pipes originally were not clamp fixed but only pushed in their support sockets.

It is clearly evident here that the engine is correctly not mounted in the centre of the frame.

FRONT FORKS

The kit parts represent the (improper for my example) early version of the front fork without the protective rubber sleeves. It is workable with internal springs interfering with its scale appearance. Thus, I decided to build a completely new version from scratch.
As again I could not rely on any drawing I scaled down a photo instead with the wheel size as the comparative measurement.
Starting with drilling the basic sections - again by the help of my handyman-drill, I finished the lower end along with the axis, spacer and front anchor plate to get the necessary width at first.
The measurement of the width gave me the opportunity to scale down pictures of the triple clamp sections. After finishing them I could fix the length of the complete front fork to make true the horizontal position of the entire model. In order to do so, at the same time I needed a new 'handle stand' for the steps to follow so I could treat the front fork parts separately and test-fit them to the model whenever necessary.

The late war BMW R75 had a large diameter front fender to prevent heavier mud from blocking the front wheel. This is not represented in the kit, but the fact that I owned two model kits made it possible to use the second sidecar fender instead, which of course made new support struts necessary also. Once the front fork was finished along with all cables and wiring it was time to go over to the sidecar assembly.

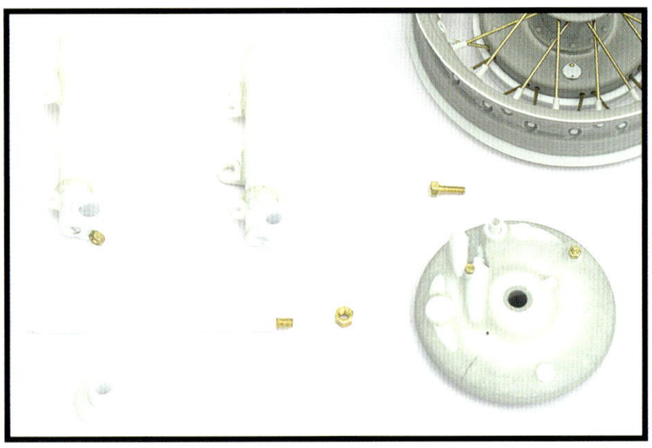

The front brake's anchor plate was the only kit part I used for the entire front fork but it needed extensive enhancement, too.

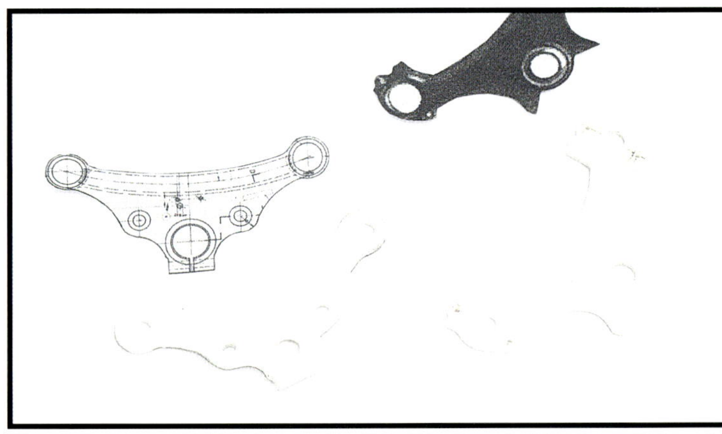

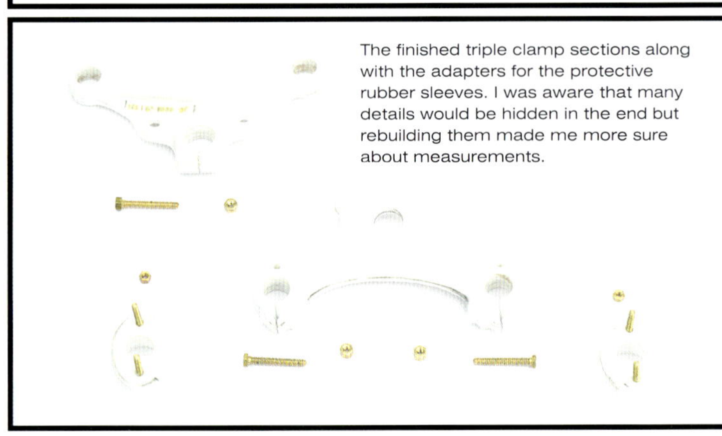

The finished triple clamp sections along with the adapters for the protective rubber sleeves. I was aware that many details would be hidden in the end but rebuilding them made me more sure about measurements.

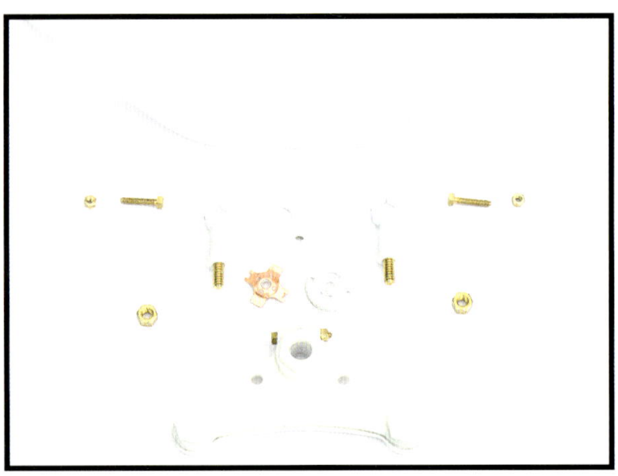

Screws and nuts made the handle bar clamps workable. This was helpful to adjust the handle bar. The latter again was made by drilled plastic rod sections with internal copper wire to allow bending and add strength. The possible length of rod to be drilled is limited of course. Notice the resulting joint in the middle.

The sidecar fender had to be cut and narrowed to represent the large diameter late type front fender
(The original front fender kit part is shown above).

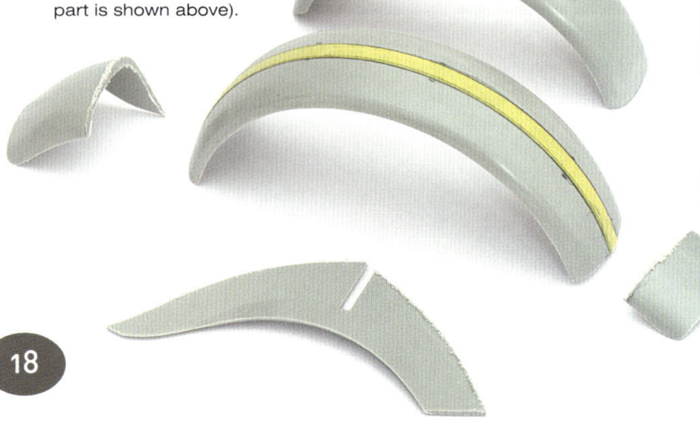

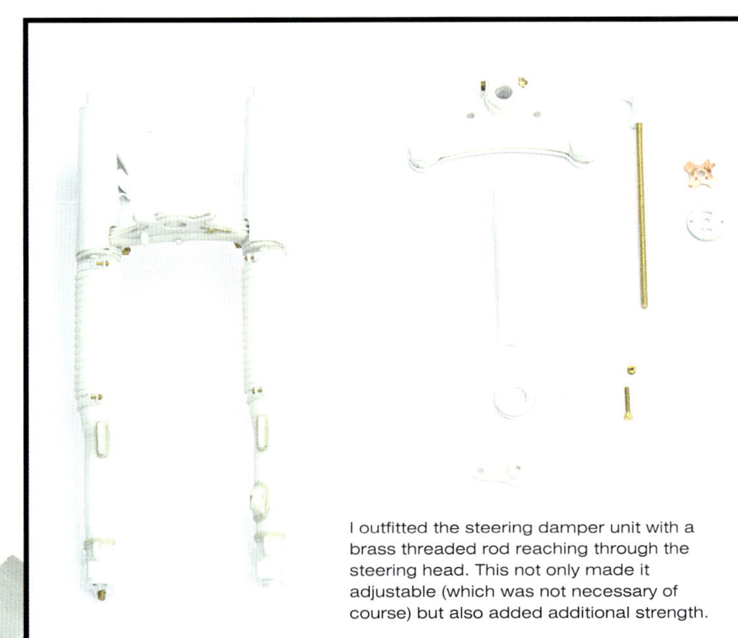

I outfitted the steering damper unit with a brass threaded rod reaching through the steering head. This not only made it adjustable (which was not necessary of course) but also added additional strength.

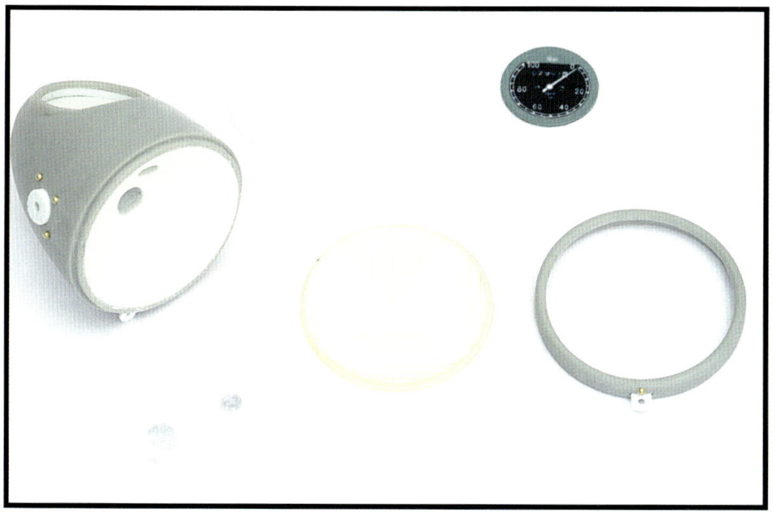

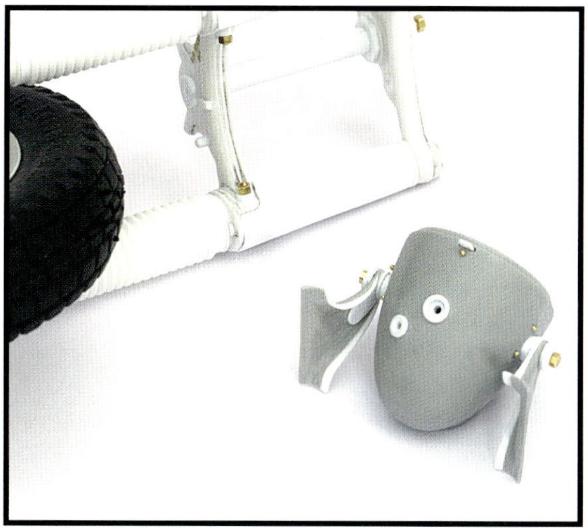

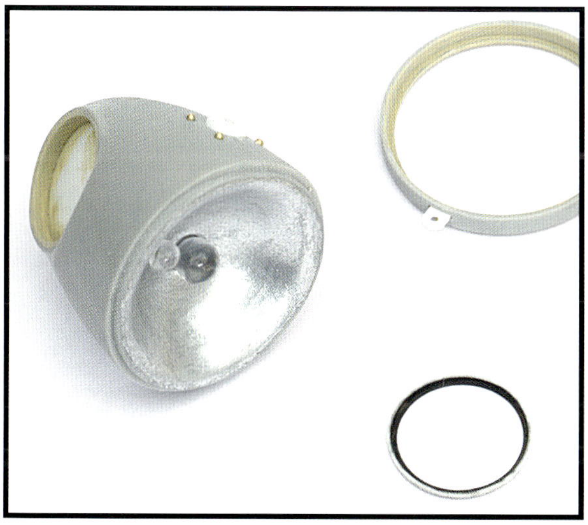

Fortunately the kit lamp body part could be used along with it's reworked fixing points. The speedometer is a made from the scaled down picture of the original. The lamp glass was made of plastic card and cast with clear resin afterwards. I had already done it for the prior Zündapp project.
The "Noris" factory marking was also carved to the inside of the glass part along with the other details in order to simplify the casting.
This would have been hiddenwith the painted version the BMW model would show. I made additional outer lettering from Magic Sculp.

The original sidecar wheel was fixed to a drive and brake system, as this keeps the level of the framework so it was possible to first simply fix the wheel to a rod pushed in the back frame tube for adapting everything to the motorcycle.

The distance between the back mounting point at the differential and the front engine mount gave me the basic measurement to scale down an exactly angled photo taken from the original parts list as a starting point. Evergreen and Plastruct plastic tubing and rod were interlocked in order to create maximum strength.
The necessary detail could be added step-by-step afterwards to this firm pre-produced base. Because the central mount for the sidecar fender was originally clamped on top of the right side leaf spring for the sidecar body, the fender was the last part to finish while working on the sidecar frame.

The kit's parts representing the side car body are far from perfect. Nevertheless, I chose to make use of them because these extremely large, softly multi-directional curved structures are really hard to build from scratch.
Unfortunately correcting (most of) the shortcomings proved pretty hard too, before I could proceed with adding the details.

Fixing the last details to the sidecar body finished the construction work on the motorcycle. Though already pretty time-consuming the main challenge was yet to come: Adapting the figures to it.

With the original motorcycle a long shaft fixed not only the split front frame parts to the front engine mount but at the same time made the main front fixing point for the sidecar frame.

In order to add maximum strength to this complex construction I used a long threaded brass rod for the same purpose replacing the plastic part that had served for fixation until this state. Some details had to be temporary removed to do so.

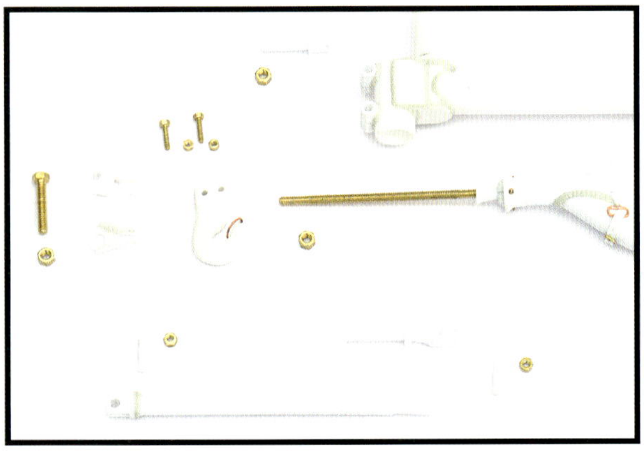

The front mount would for sure be one of the most critical points when adding the heavy figures to the sidecar. Therefore I made the threaded brass rod reaching into the originally adjustable sidecar's front mount.

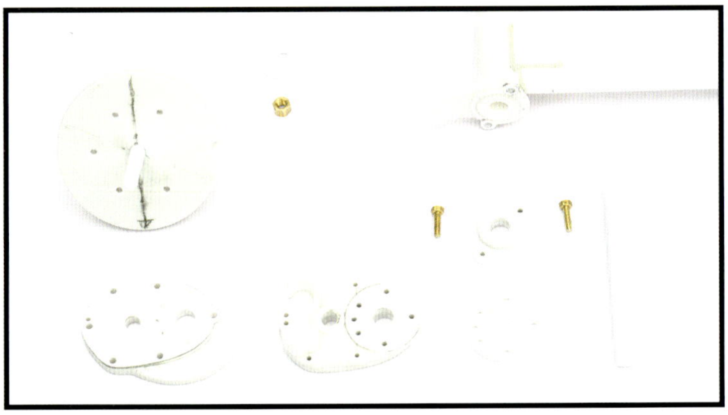

Originally the sidecar wheel was suspended along with the complete sidecar drive/brake-unit by a torsion bar located in the back sidecar frame tube. I finally made a slotted brass screw fixing the complete unit, which also would have to withstand the rather heavy weight.

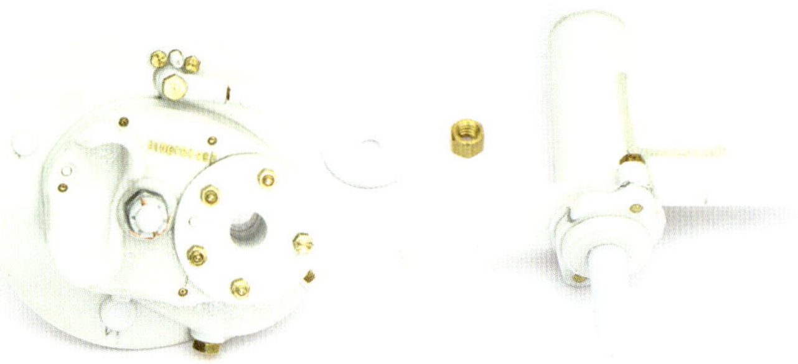

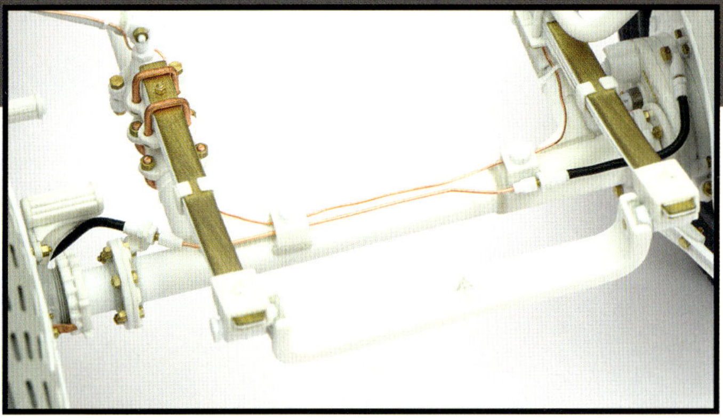

The rigid brake line for the side car wheel is running along the electric wiring for the side car position light. The soft sections are made of electric cable, which is rather easy to adapt due to the internal copper wire. All connecting parts were drilled from Plastruct hexagonal material and outfitted with inner threads and an internal threaded brass rod.

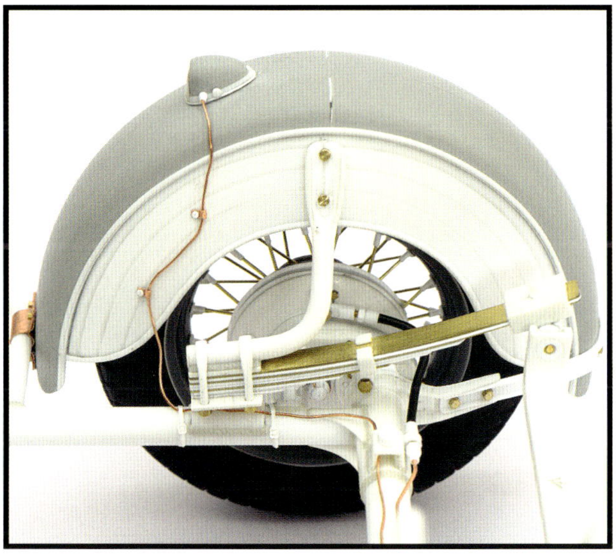

The middle fender support was the last item I finished. With earlier versions an additional electric wire ran from the front to the rear position light. Notice how the necessary gap in the front light body was just closed with a blanking plug.

Three of the nine elements of the leaf spring support for the sidecar body were made of brass strips for strengthening purposes.

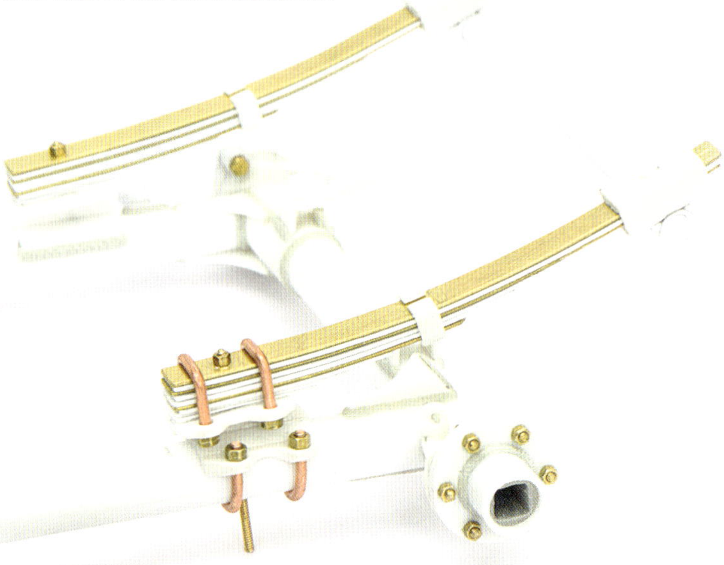

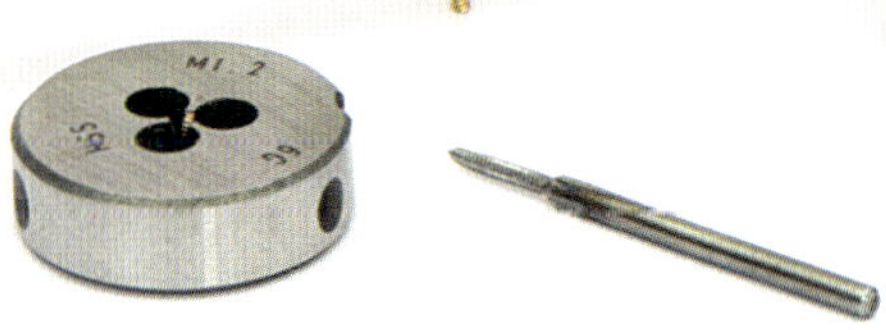

I cut threads to the copper wire sections of the clamp mechanism for the leaf spring support which made it a secure strong point already. Additionally I made the threaded brass rods originally only holding the leaf spring sections themselves reaching through the complete sidecar frame.

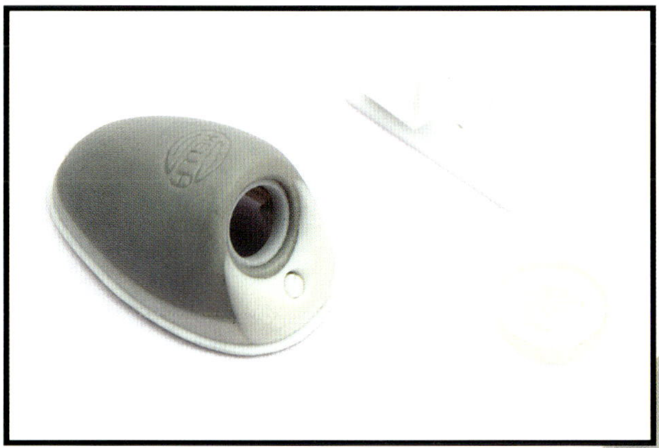

The fender position-light body is marked as “Hella” produced, the lens comes from “Noris” instead. I had already cast the latter from clear resin for my former Zündapp project. The additional rear fender light was dropped with the late-production BMW R75.

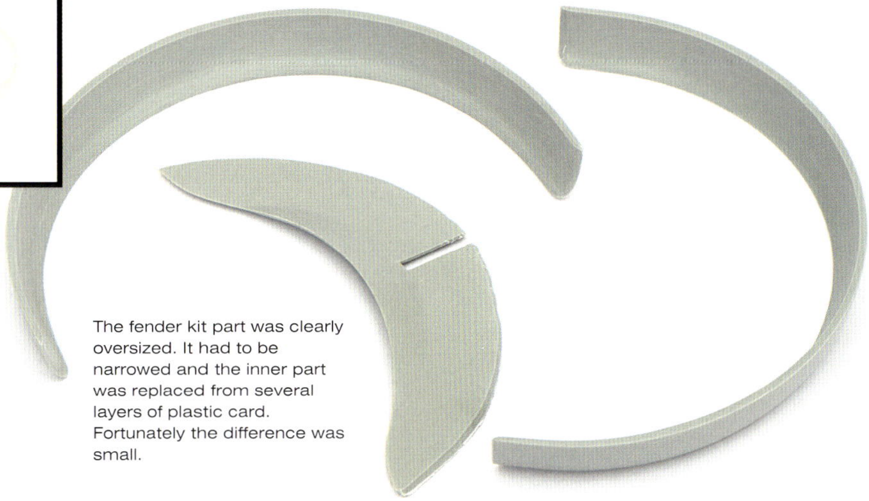

The fender kit part was clearly oversized. It had to be narrowed and the inner part was replaced from several layers of plastic card. Fortunately the difference was small.

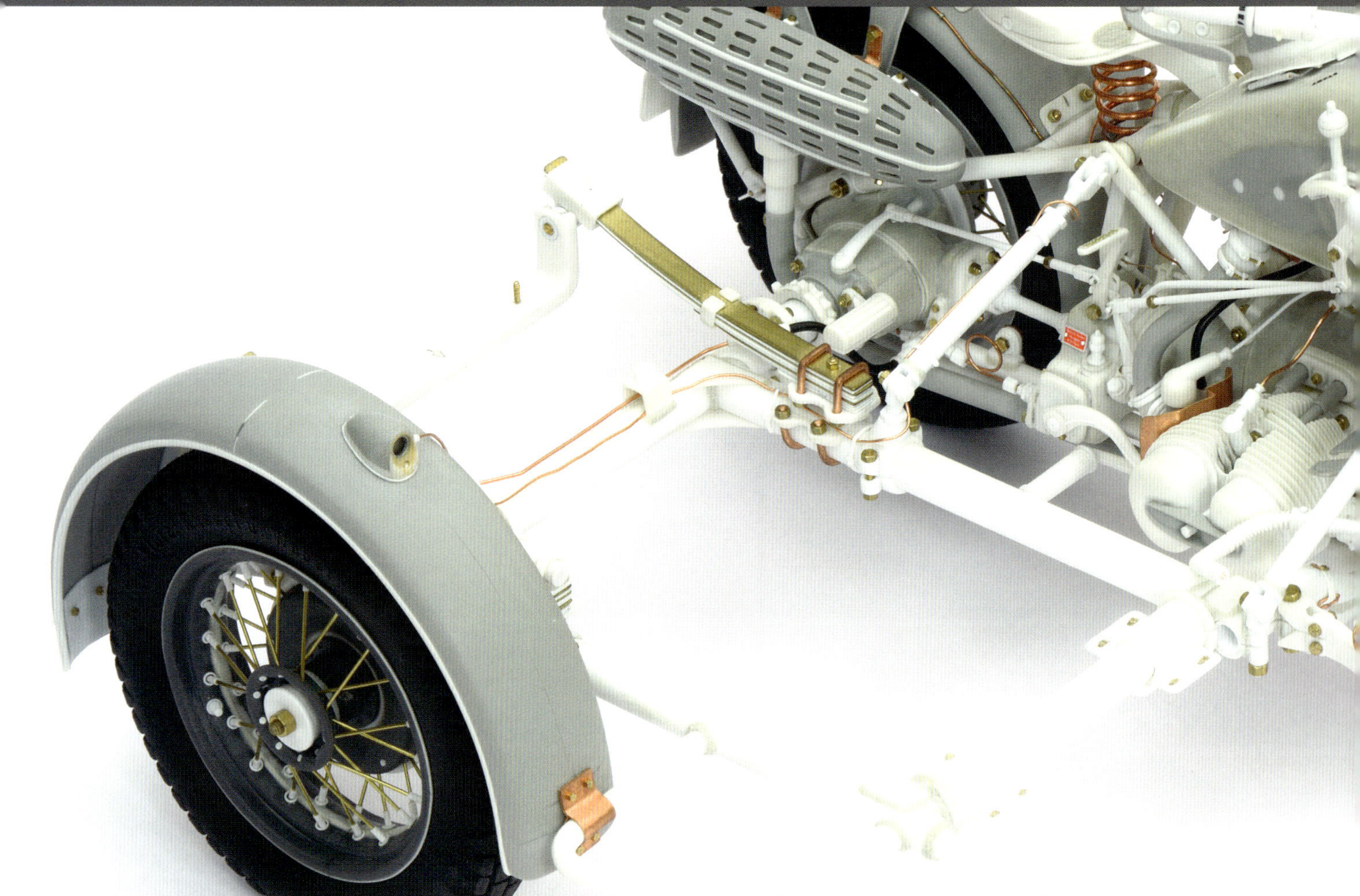

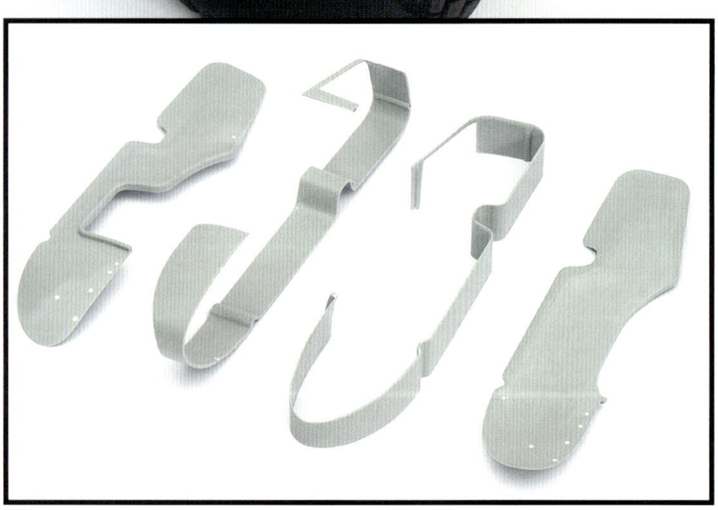

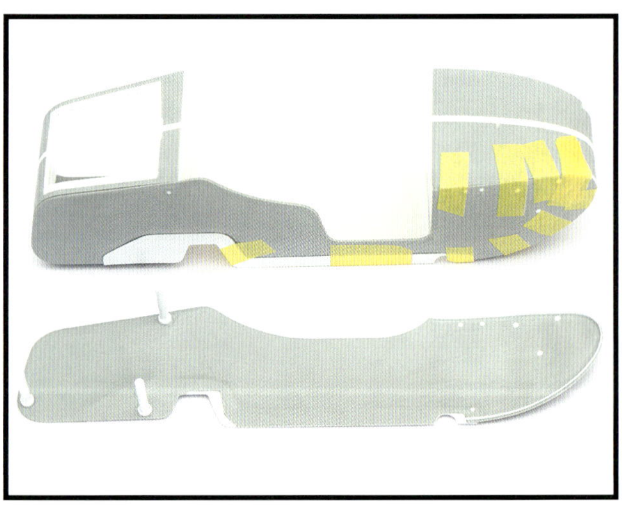

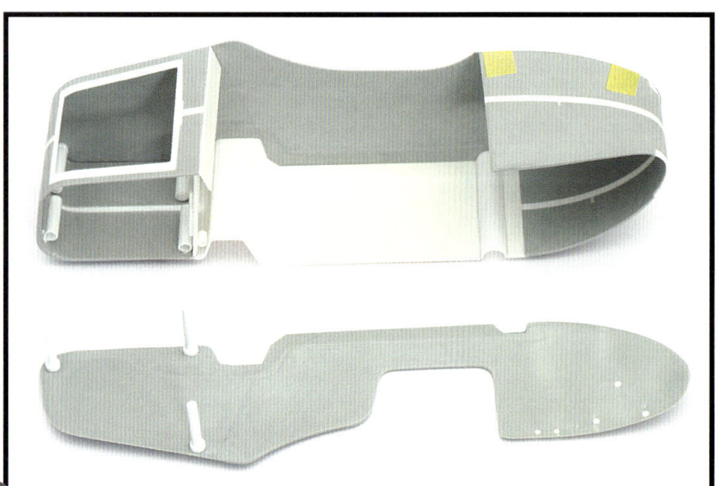

The kit part is simply split in half. This makes it just impossible to hide the central joint as some areas have to be painted before final assembly. So I decided to change the kit part layout by cutting-off the sidewalls.
The lower cut-outs of sidewalls had to be adapted to the prepared sidecar frame.

Originally the sidecar body front was secured by an internal frame. With the model just the opposite is true; I used the test-fitted body sections to add the comparably delicate frame. The strengthening tubes on the edges were again bent by the help of internal copper wire.

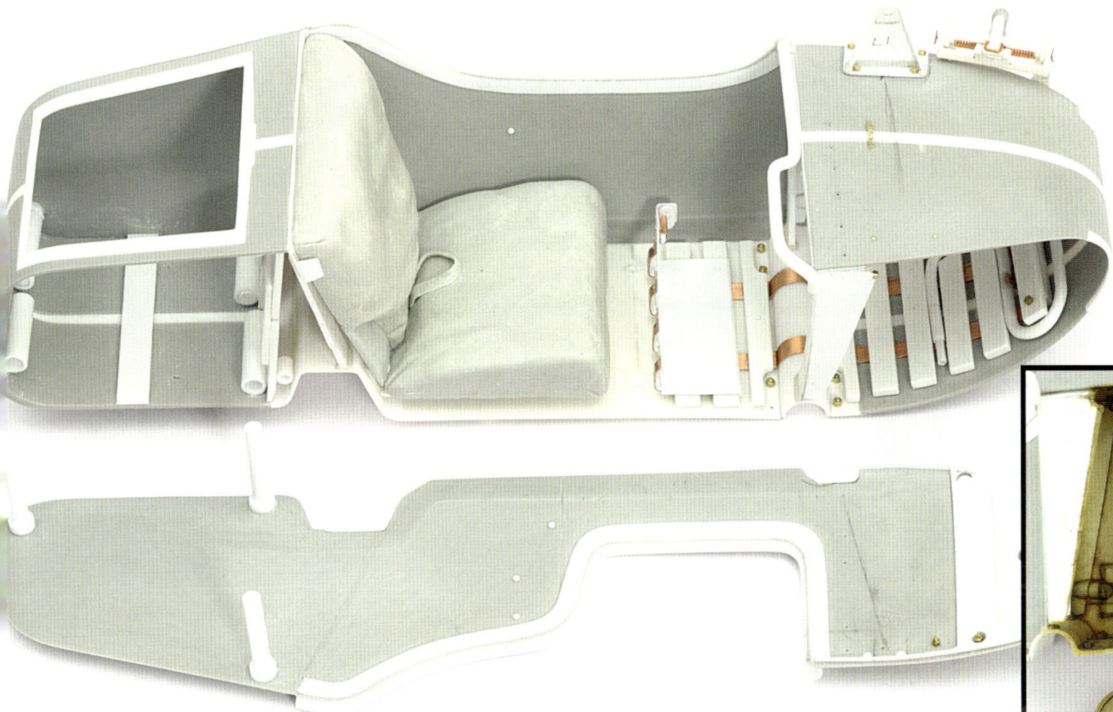

In 1942 a heating system for the driver's hands and feet as well as the sidecar foot space was introduced. While the driver's heating devices were later on dropped as they did not prove effective, the heating system for the sidecar stayed an ongoing serial addition. It was closely adapted to the wooden foot rest sections and fixed to the sheet metal flooring.

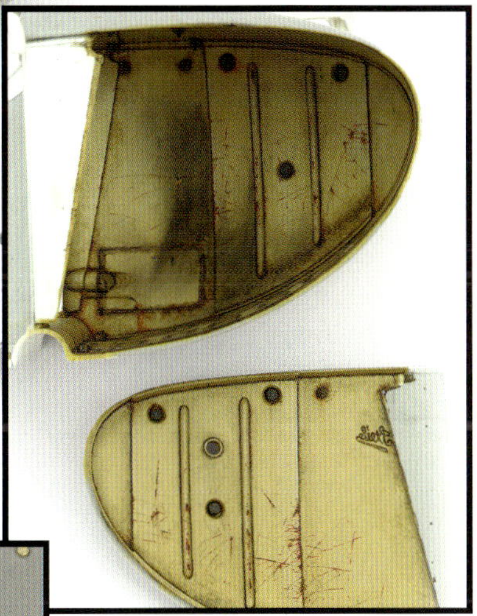

As the foot space would be out of reach after gluing the right sidewall it needed a complete painting and weathering treatment beforehand. Notice the mirrored carved "Steib" factory logo originally pressed into the sheet metal.

I made the fixing clamp securing the MG34 a working mechanism; not necessary of course but a nice gimmick to end the construction work with it.
The height and the side position of the MG34 mount could be adjusted and the whole mechanism could be turned around for left hand use.

I made two versions of the sidecar seat. One served to create a complete looking finished version and one to later adapt the figures. Both were fixed with small but amazingly strong magnets.
The finished interior below. The structure in front of the seat served to fix a standard rack for two drum magazines of the MG34.

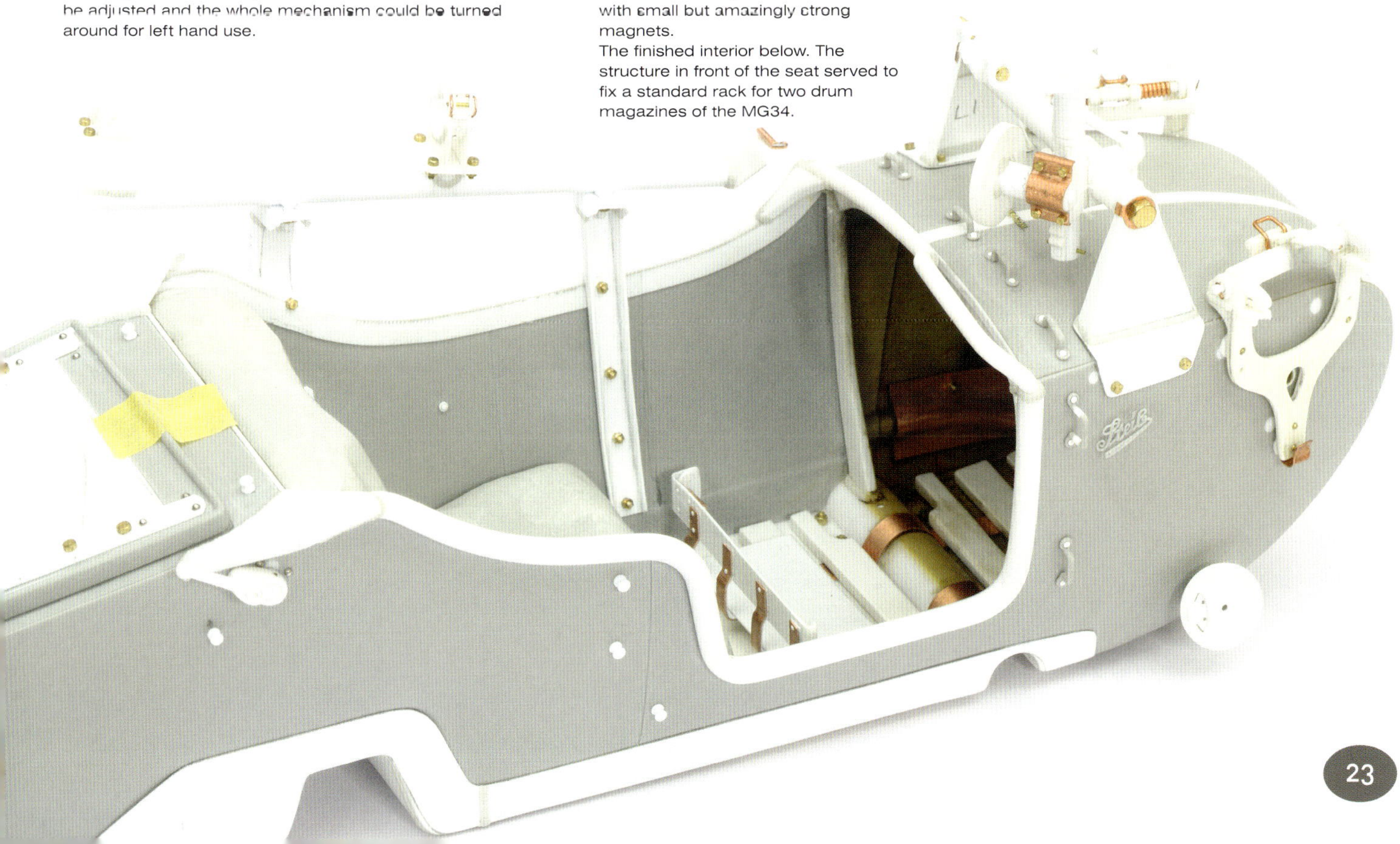

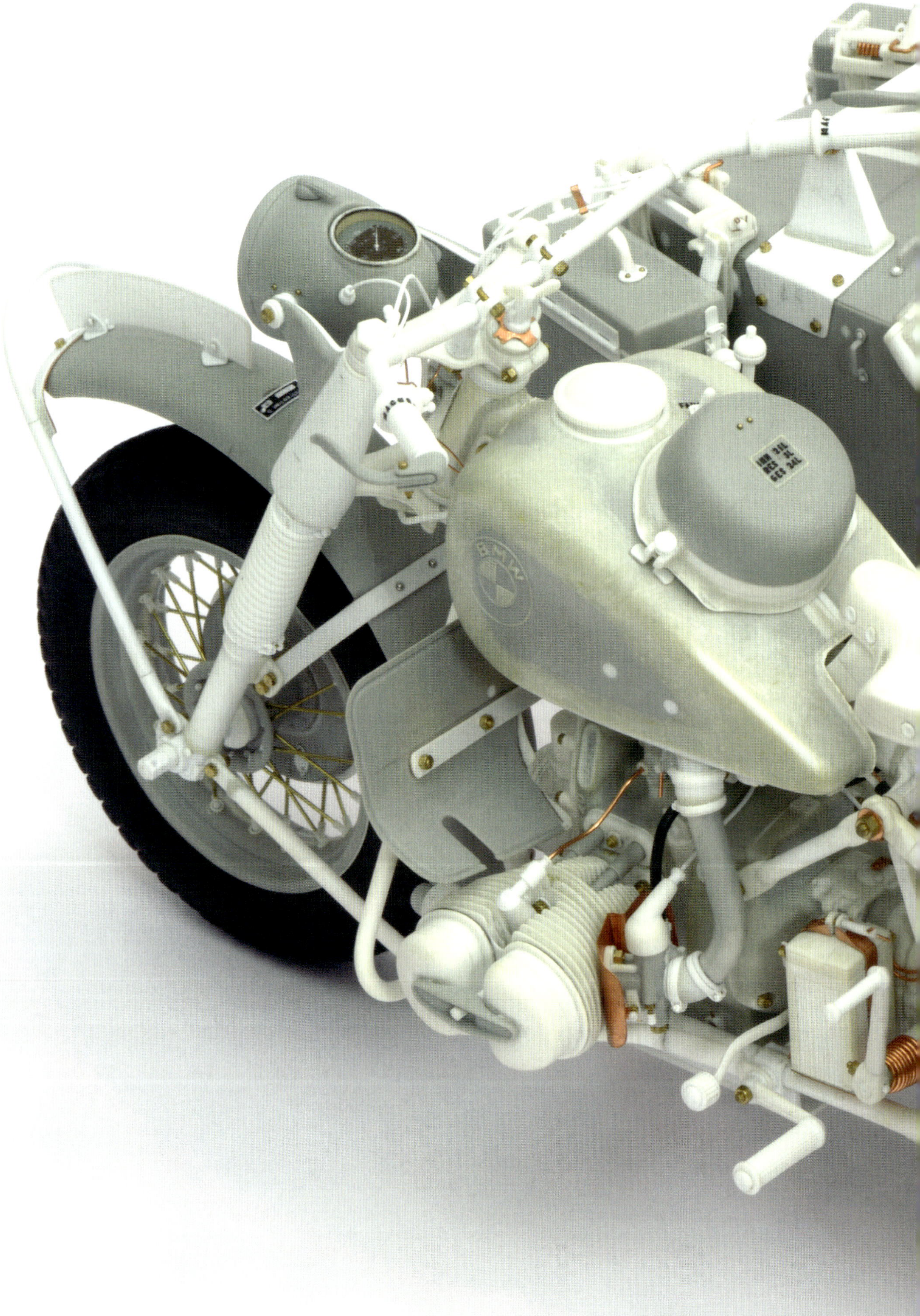
BMW

Drilastic
Drilastic

Like with the original the front wheel is neither in the middle of the front fork nor in the middle of the fender. Otherwise it would not been possible to remove it with the pumped-up tyre in place.

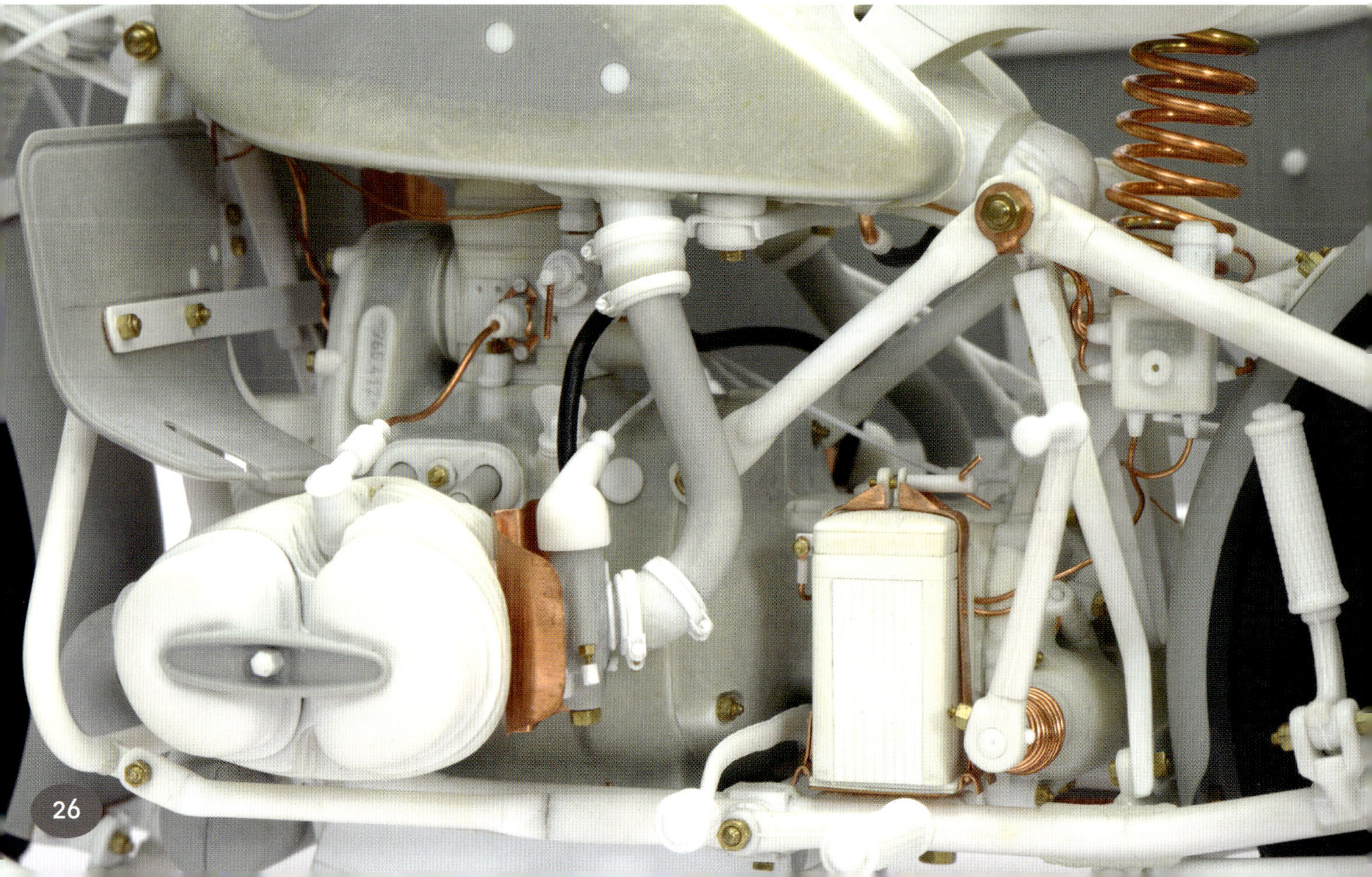

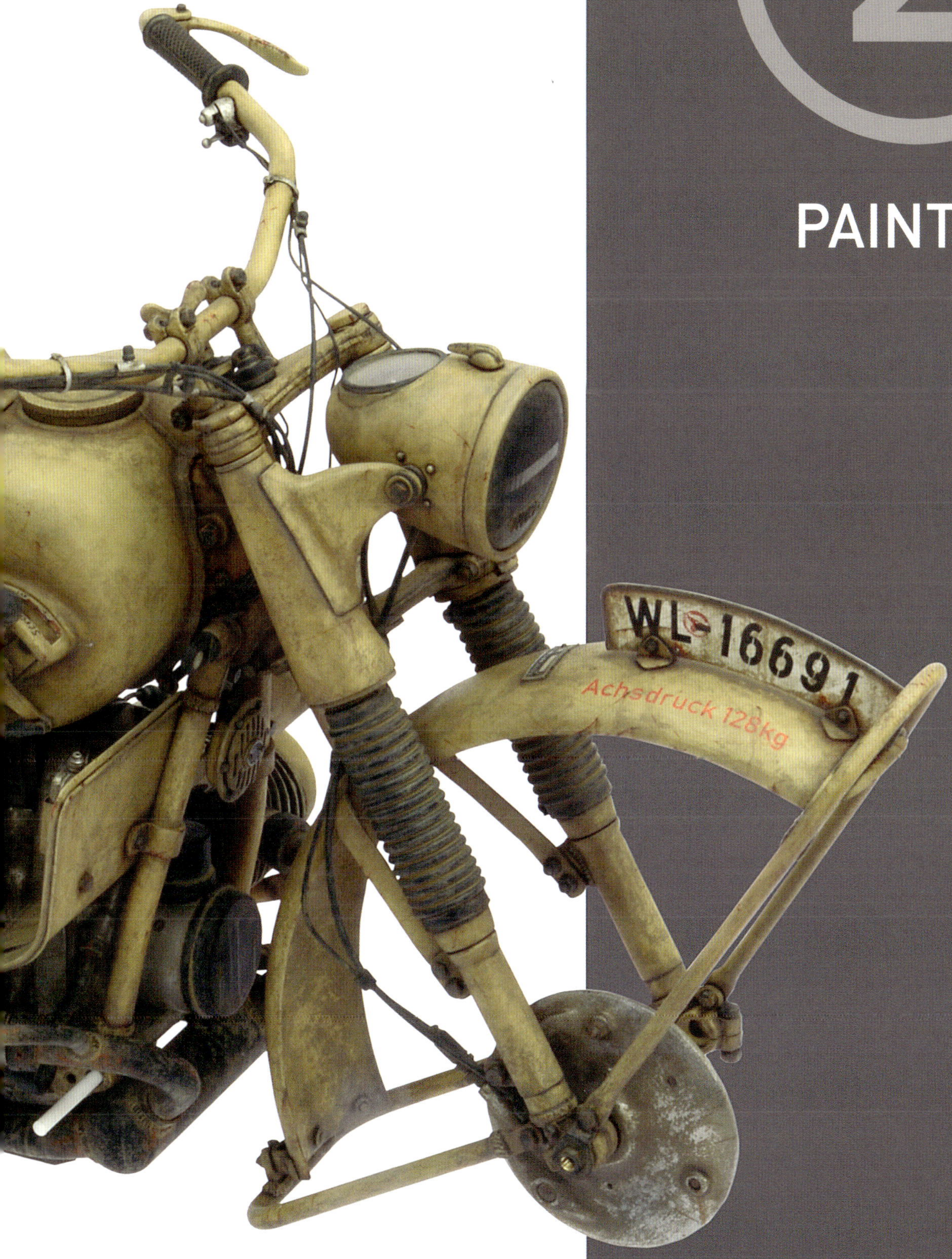

2

PAINTING

BASE COLOURS

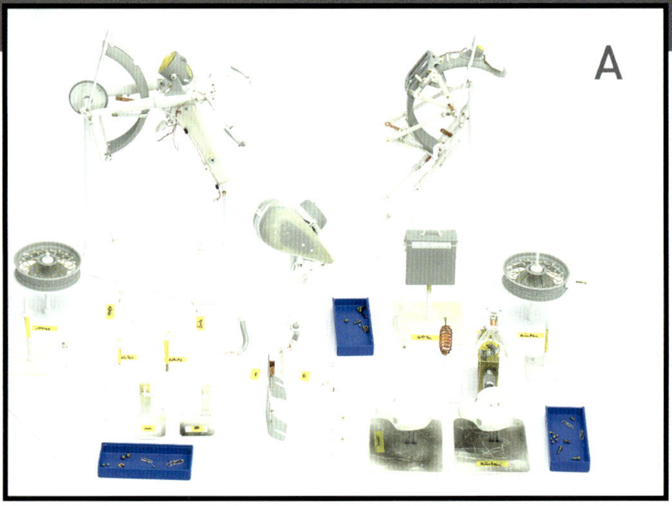

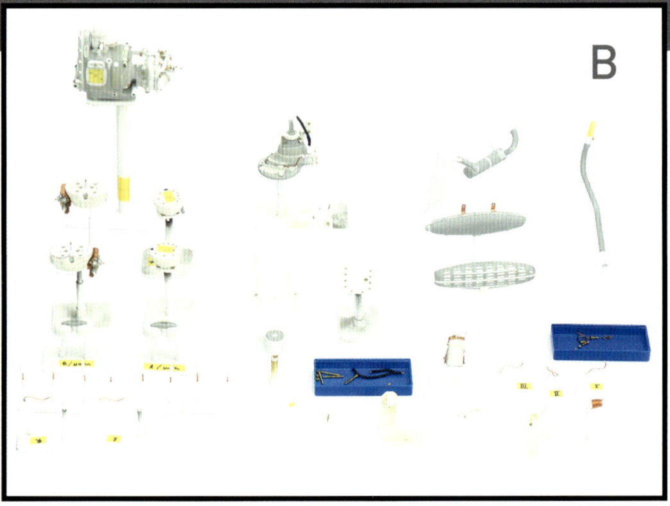

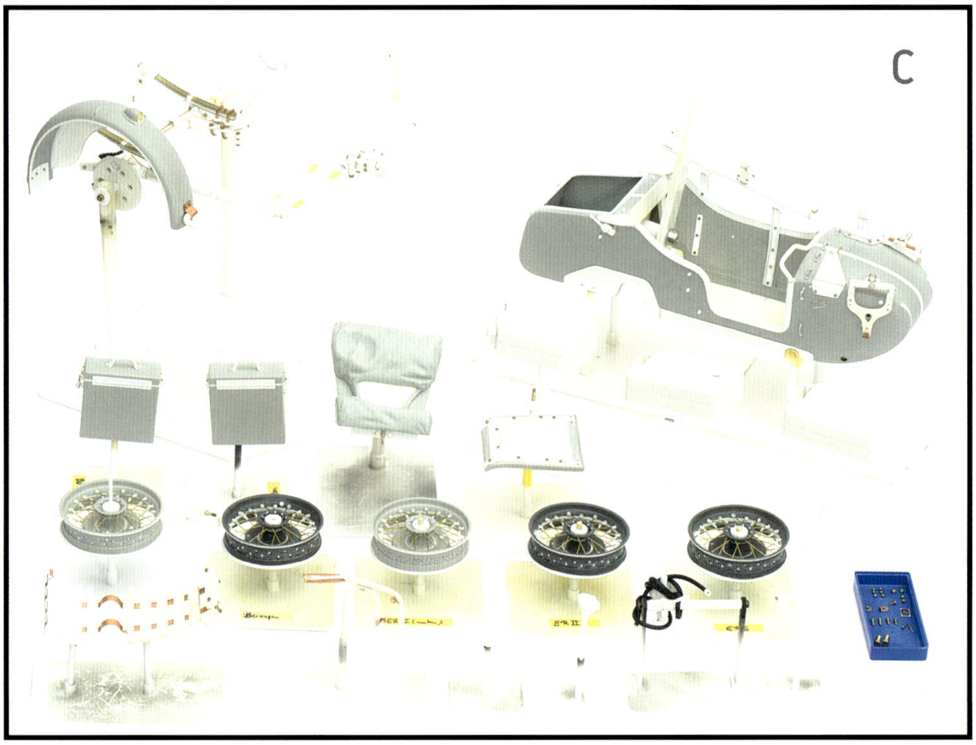

The pictures show the parts for the motorcycle minus the engine parts (A), the engine parts with all technical additions (B) and the sidecar assembly (C). Many parts had to be marked to avoid mixing them up.

It is very hard to estimate the colouration of items shown in black and white photographs. The task is even complicated with the photo I have chosen as a model because the motorcycle and soldiers are obviously covered with dirt and the photo was taken in poor lighting conditions. This effect pursued me during every decision on the painting.

The fact that many sub-assemblies were screw fixed allowed to disassemble the model to a high degree. I did not follow a fixed plan but just tried to keep the sub-assemblies as large as possible while allowing me to reach every area. This resulted in a fair amount of separated items which all were fitted to home-made handles in order to allow painting without touching the cleaned-up model parts.
I used white-coloured Mr. Paint primer to make mistakes apparent and provide a proper adhesion on the metal parts in particular. Once this preliminary work had been done I had to finally decide about the basic colour tones.
The main colour seems to be the standard "Dunkelgelb" (dark yellow).

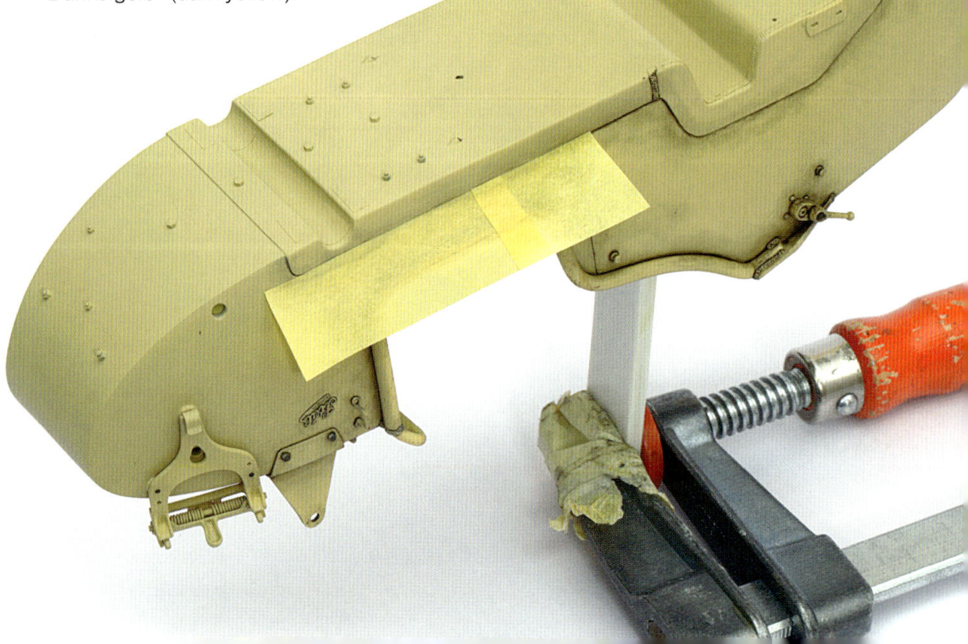

The outer stowage box is very dark so I decided to paint it in "Dunkelgrau" (dark grey). The inner one seems to be dark compared to the sidecar body also but this effect is very subtle at least compared to the fuel tank - but not to the lamp body and front fender; I painted it with primer red instead.
I chose to use straight black for the likely paint covered headlight lens, but it looks rather light compared to the outer stowage box, but compared to the gas cables and the rubber of the fork's protective sleeves... well, in the end some decisions had to be taken accepting that there was more than one way to go!
All camouflage colours were mixed from the Tamiya acrylic range. Unfortunately all of them have kind of "grown" through the years and I can't tell exactly the mixing ratios.
But to be honest, I am always amused by heated discussions by modellers about the correct colour mixtures keeping in mind that there is no way to find out exactly about how colours may have appeared 80 years ago and original relics seem to vary greatly. In addition their model representations will be affected not only by the scale but by the differing weathering effects as well.
I chose to spend some money on markings perfectly custom-made following my literature based guidelines by the German company Tailormadedecals.

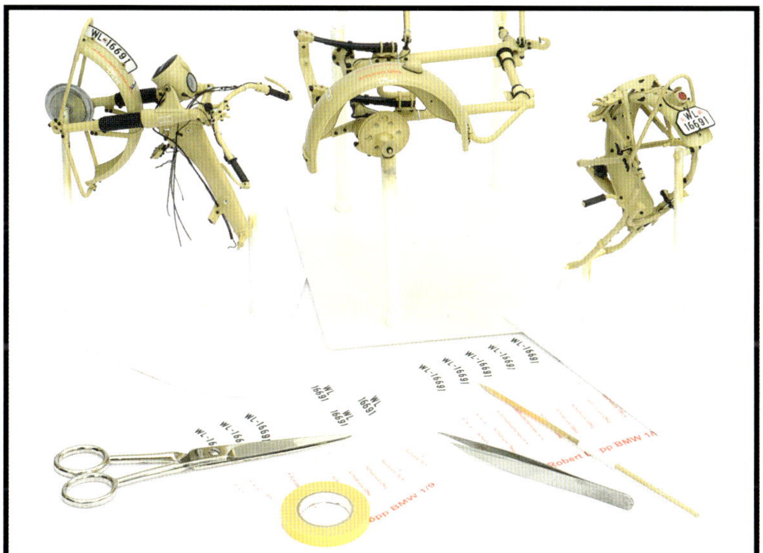

The custom made Tailormadedecals markings were of dry-transfer type. They worked best on a shiny surface achieved with a layer of Tamiya "Clear" (X-22).

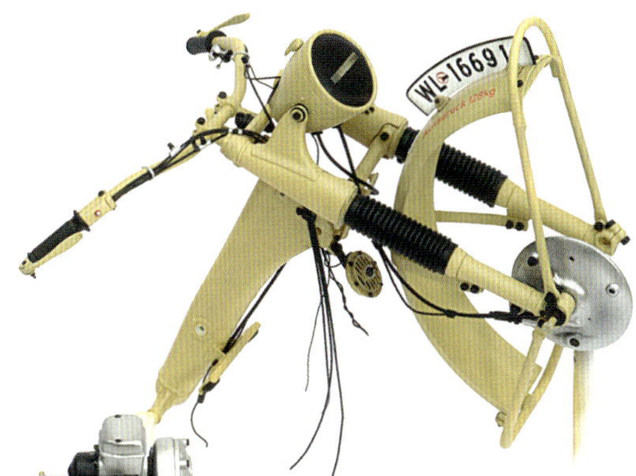

I made use of Vallejo "White Aluminum" for the originally rough cast larger parts and straight "Aluminum" for the more delicate ones like the carbs and fuel tap.

Not every BMW R75 (nor Zündapp KS750) carried the transport markings for weight and measurements but they surely add to the impression of detail and refinement so I decided to use them.
It is hard to say how the aluminum-cast parts may have originally looked, because restored parts usually are polished by a wire brush, creating extra shine, or glass bead blasted changing the surface.
Differing from my former Zündapp models I decided to use silver shades from the Vallejo "Metal Colour" range this time as I was after the extra contrast to the flat dust and dirt adhesions.
In the end everything was sealed with Tamiya semi-satin acrylic varnish (X-22/X-21) to be safe from disturbance by the following weathering process.

WEATHERING

As far as I am concerned "weathering" a scale model should not only just try to mimic natural effects but keep in mind the appearance of the scale result. Therefore, while proceeding I have tried to create an interesting looking three-dimensional effect with deepened shadows and highlights and preserve a refined detailed look avoiding ending up in a mess.
The first step was a "washing" treatment with white spirit diluted oil paints. The necessary darkening effect was partly compensated by a "dry-brushing" run with light oil paint

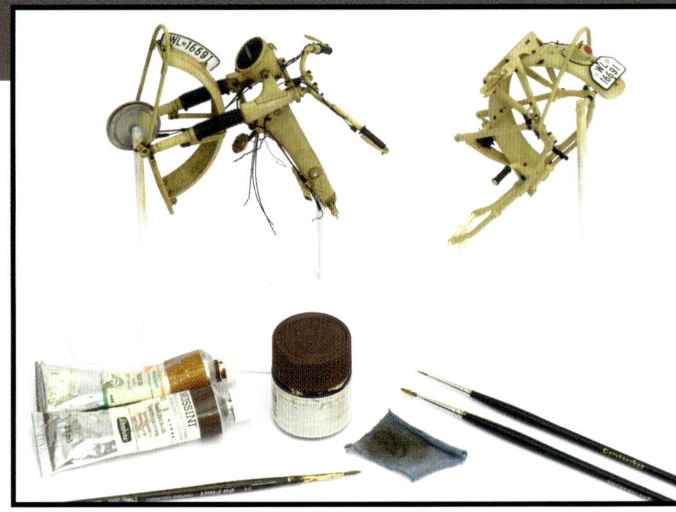

The dark "wash" was mixed in an approximately 50/50 ratio of Raw Umber and Vandyke Brown. Every detail was outlined and the transitions were feathered with white-spirit moistened brushes whenever necessary. I carefully treated all surfaces with an extra diluted mix also in order to create an already used and dirty overall appearance. The right half is still untreated above.

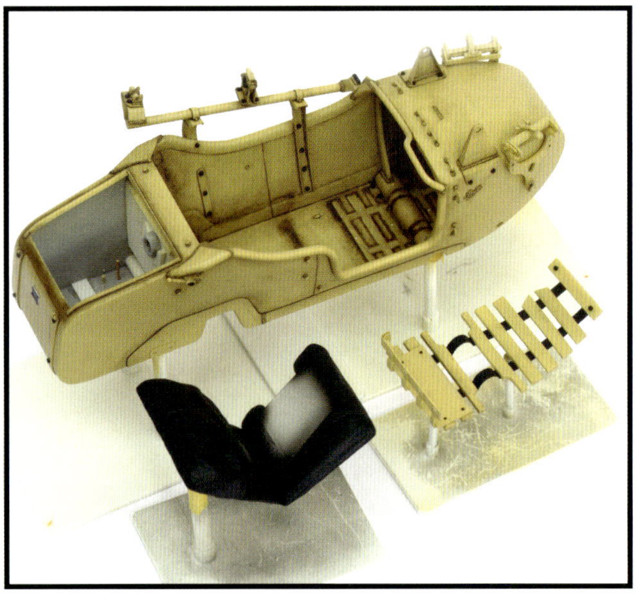

The still lose internal components of the sidecar had to be temporary inserted for creating an adapted outlining effect.

Adding some highlights with 502 Abteilung "Buff" compensated the darkening effect partially and helped to add depth. Again the right half stayed untreated for the picture.

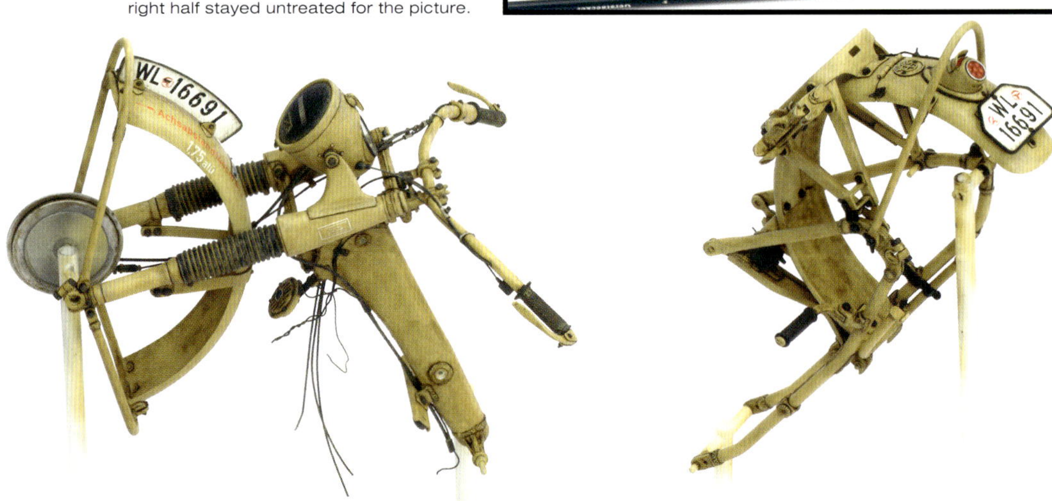

The black parts received a dusty light "wash" mixed from white-spirit diluted Italian Earth and 502 Abteilung "Light Mud" oils instead. Only the left half is finished here for comparison.

The oil-paint based brush applied chipping was followed by adding streaks from varying rusty tones around the areas representing bare metal.
In order to adapt the heavily weathered look of the motorcycle I tried to create the effect of partly washed off layers of dust and dirt with highly diluted brown tones of Revell enamels sprayed onto a preparing layer of AK-Interactive "Worn Effects" and partially removed it with varying water-moistened brushes.
On the "Dunkelgelb" parts I chose a comparably dark earth tone and concentrated a still translucent layer on the lower parts because I wanted to preserve the shadowing and the delicate effects of the preceding weathering steps.
Throughout the whole process I had to deal with the fact that all subunits had to be treated separately at first, partially assembled during progress and harmonized in the end without losing too much contrast. In particular the interior of the sidecar body had to be finished before the underside of the body could be sprayed and weathered and the heated engine parts received an extra rust-treatment before the whole power train assembly could be dusted as well.

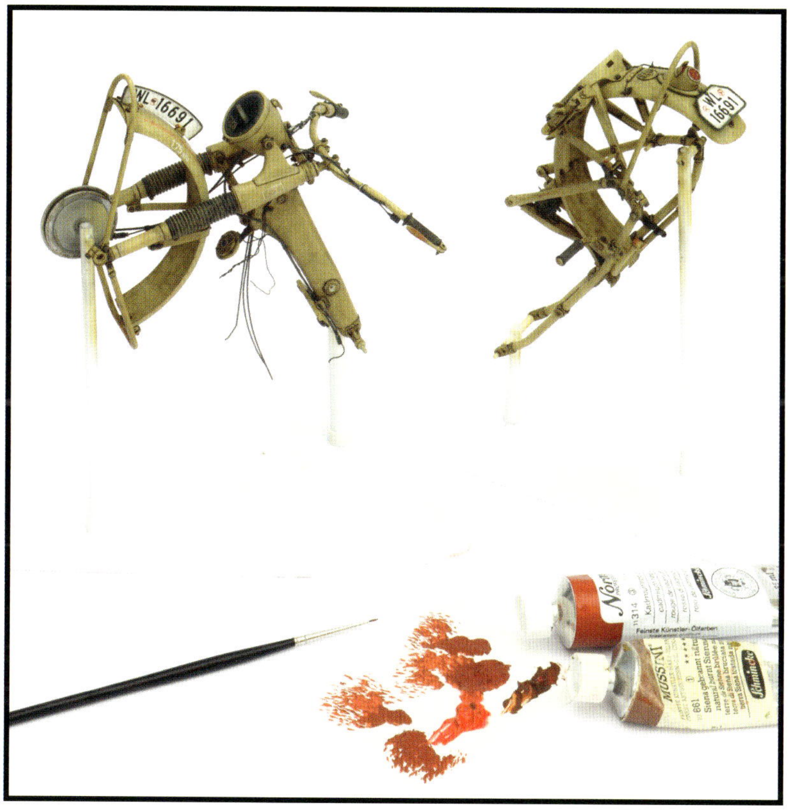

A first chipping-run mimicked areas of primer red showing through. The paint was mixed from Natural Burnt Sienna and Cadmium Red oils very slightly diluted with linseed oil.
Chips and scratches showing bare metal were mimicked with a dark grey mix from linseed oil diluted Mars Black and Titanium White oils.

Most of the streaking was done with 502 Abteilung "Brown Wash", which creates a convincing "pre-rusted" look. Only a few areas were treated with varying rusty tones mixed from Natural Burnt Sienna and Chrome Orange oils. All of them were white-spirit diluted and feathered with more white spirit.
On all "Dunkelgelb" parts I used Revell "Dark-Earth" (Matt 87). It is hard to control the applied amount of the clear chipping fluid, which makes the effect hard to control as well. That is why it proved best to start with a soft brush only slightly moistened with water and going over to more water and stiffer bristles whenever necessary.

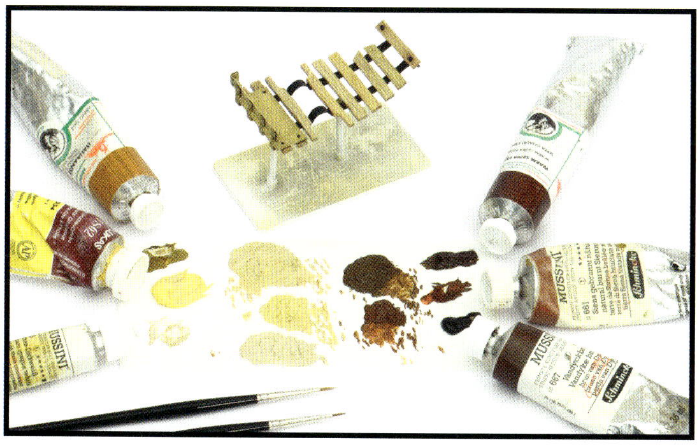

The wooden planks of the foot rest were painted with varying oil mixes applying a light shade (Titanium Opaque White/Italian Earth/Naples Yellow Light) and a significantly darker one (Warm Sepia Extra/Natural Burnt Sienna/Vandyke Brown) in a wet-on-wet mode partially mixing them in order to create a varying wood grain pattern.

Similar to the "dust"-application the wooden parts were weathered with a very thin layer of black Revell enamel sprayed onto pre-applied AK-Interaktive "Worn Effects" and removed with water-moistened brushes.

The foot rest had to be completely finished along with the heating tube section before it could be screwed into the sidecar body. After that, the latter could finally be sprayed from the underside as well.

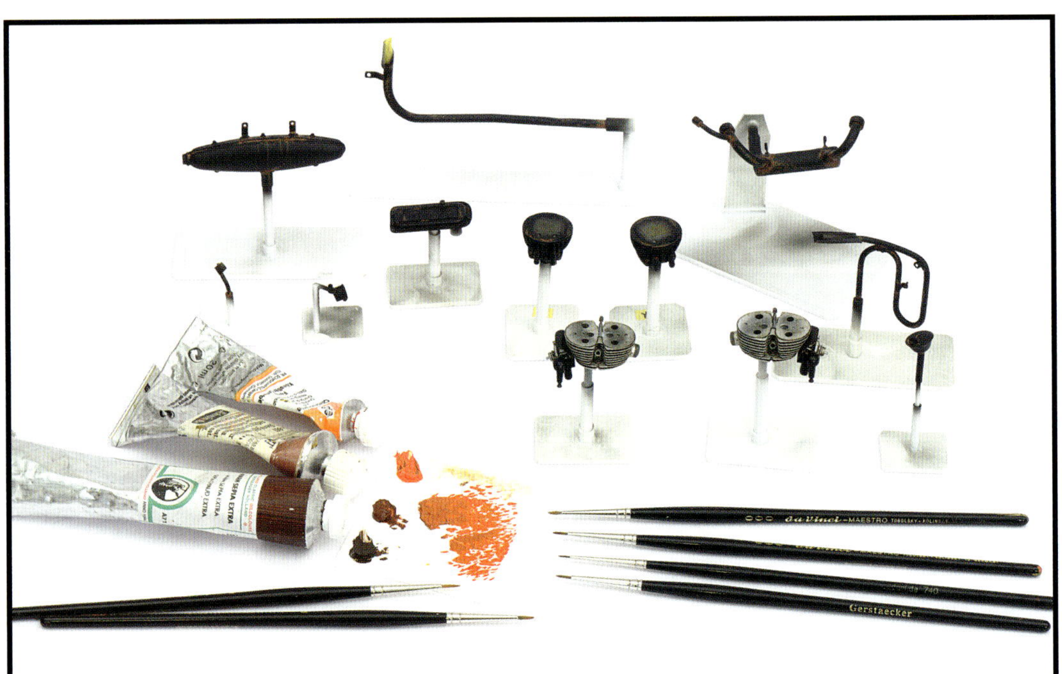

The frequently heated iron-based engine parts were originally sealed with a heat-resistant black paint. Nevertheless they certainly collected rust marks in some heavily affected areas. I mimicked this effect with varying mixes of Chrome Orange, Natural Burnt Umber and Warm Sepia Extra oils representing rust of differing age and intensity.

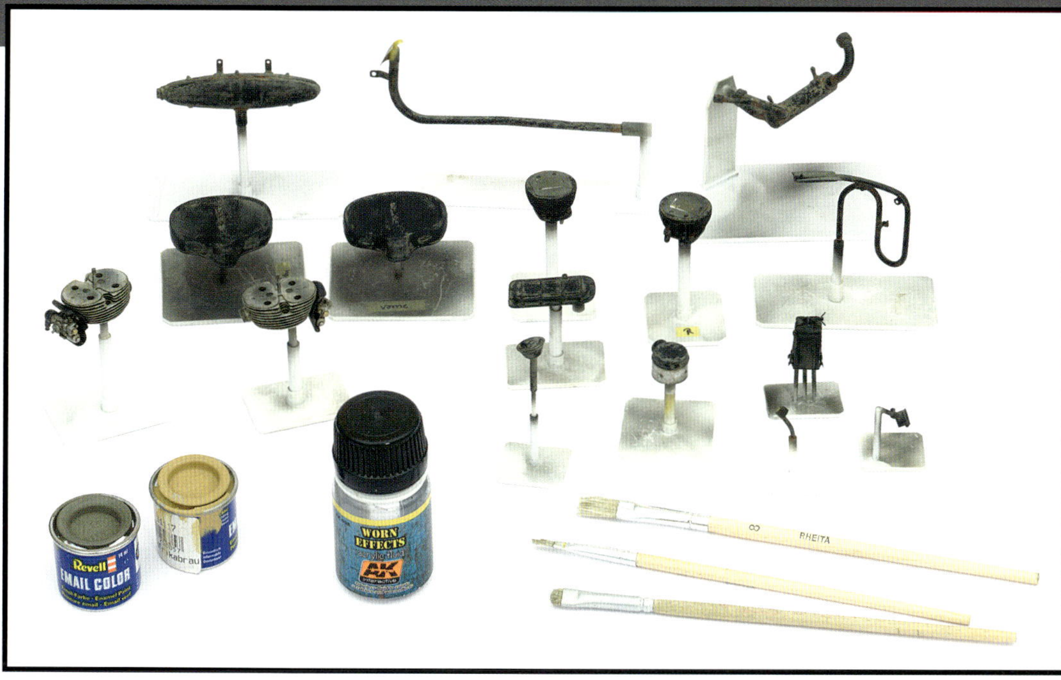

A dust treatment similar to the one added to the entire "Dunkelgelb" surfaces was added to the partially pre-rusted black parts as well but based on a lighter shade of Revell enamels mixed from "Dark Earth" (Matt 87) and "Africa Brown" (Matt 17).

The sidecar MG34 mount was originally delivered in a blackened condition but it seems to show an irregular light shade in the photo instead. Maybe the main part has been salvaged from another motorcycle?! Thus I have decided to cover it with a variation of "Dunkelgelb" heavily chipped by the help of pre-applied AK-Interactive´s "Worn Effects". The fuel hose was covered with "Maskol" from Humbrol.

The main mud mix was made of brown oil colour shades (Natural Burnt Umber/502 Abteilung “Light Mud”/Italian Earth/Naples Yellow Light) and pigments (Cyprus Umber/Mig-Productions “Europe Dust”).

Some modelling grass helped to add texture. Once dry some areas of the model were carefully matted with Model Master “Flat Clear” in order to avoid shiny rust, dust and dirt representations.

Fresh, semi-satin mud was represented by a darker mixture instead; Vandyke Brown and Italian Earth oils mixed with Cassel Brown pigments.

The hard to control chipped dust effect was corrected and enhanced with light dusty oil paint shades diluted with white spirit. The result is exemplified by the rubber tires. In this case the dust “wash” picks out the factory tire markings in particular. The right wheel has not been treated yet. Notice the threaded brass rod already screwed into an internal plastic thread, which will later on fix the model firmly to the base.

All four spare wheels. Only the upper one shows adequate wheel hub detail as all others were to be completely hidden in the end, unfortunately a lot of extra work on the spokes and tyres would be as well!

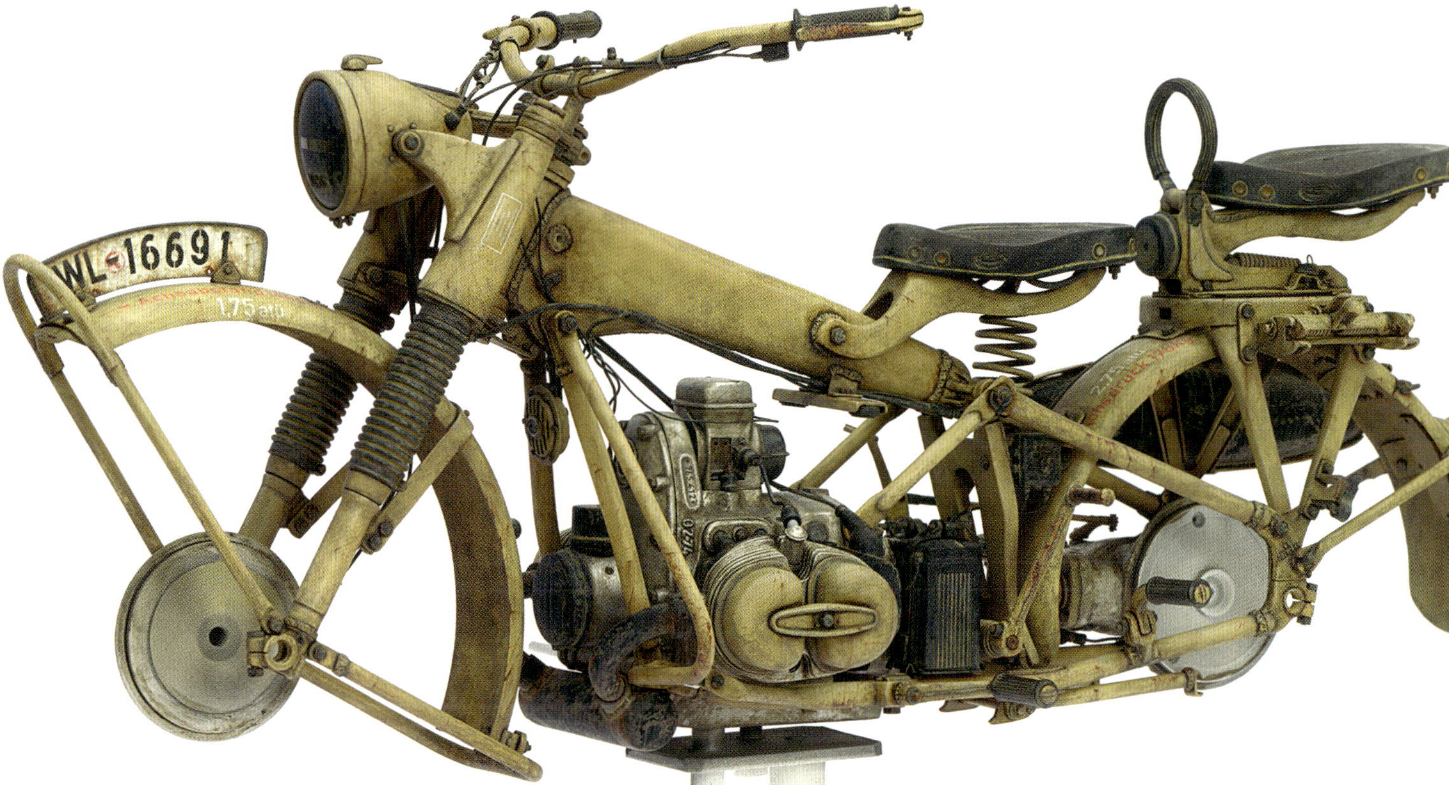

Fixing the engine along with all additional components into the frame while assembling it was the first challenging step to take. Notice the electric wiring in particular.

Mixing small amounts of Raw Umber oils with natural turpentine will result in a semi-satin thin fluid adequate for the representation of fuel stains. Adding some white-spirit will minimize the shine. Adding more Raw Umber and Titanium Black oils with linseed oil can be used for oily remains of different ages. Adding megilp (oil painting 'gel') to the mix achieves a thick greasy consistency.

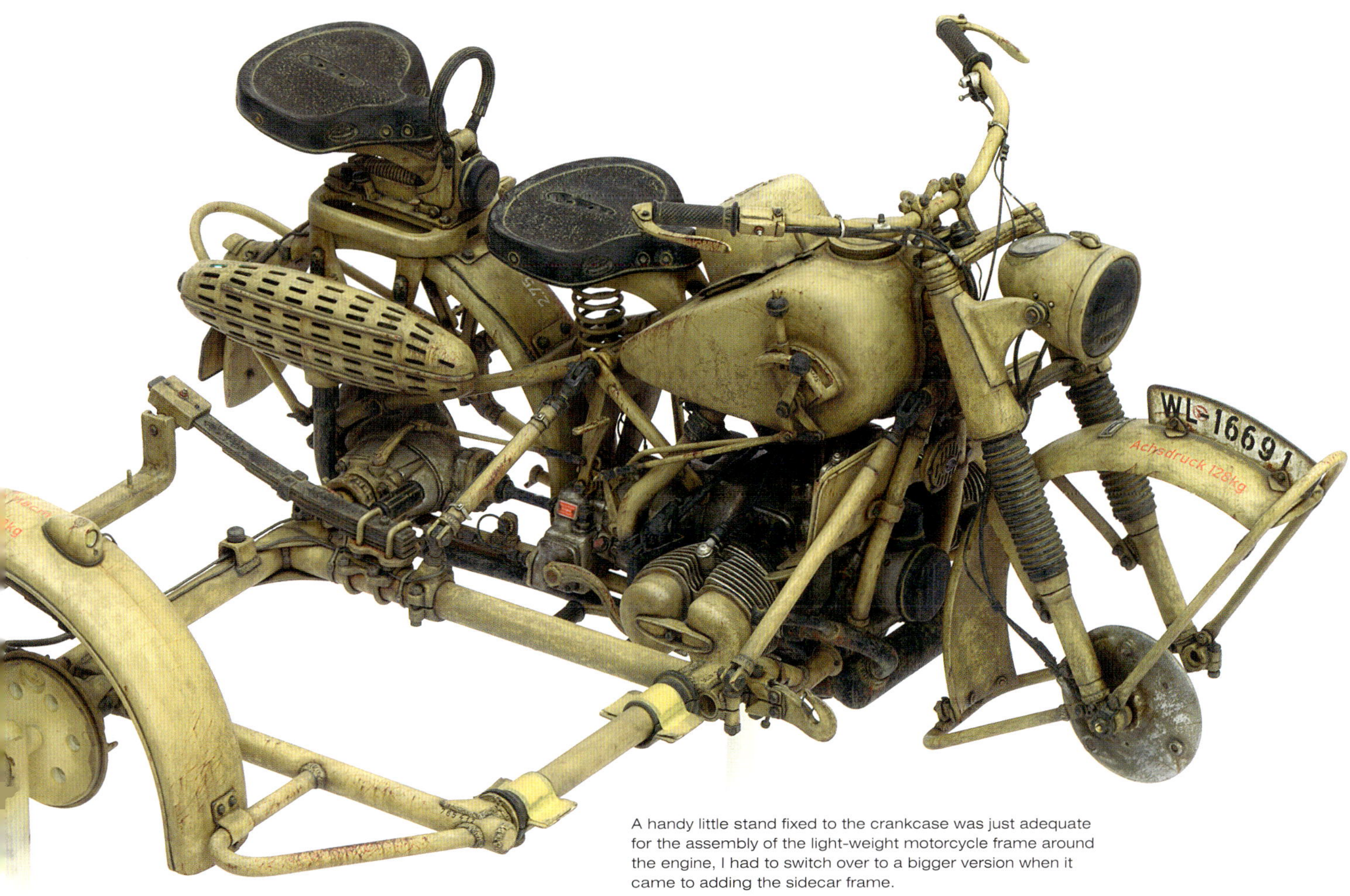

A handy little stand fixed to the crankcase was just adequate for the assembly of the light-weight motorcycle frame around the engine, I had to switch over to a bigger version when it came to adding the sidecar frame.

I have learned from H.P. Hommes that the screws and bolts on German vehicles were usually "atramentiert" (atramented) resulting in an off-black phosphate layer that sealed the material fast and easily but not really perfectly.
Initially on motorcycles the pre-painted parts were assembled and received a second paint-layer afterwards including most of the connection parts. But the standards were lowered later on in order to save time and material so that many connective parts stayed untreated like they had always been on the unpainted technical parts also.

Therefore I painted all screw and connective parts on the entire motorcycle black. All the brass parts that I had kept separated for the final assembly were blackened with burnishing fluid but the resulting surface proved extremely delicate. So all parts had to be painted, received a dusty "wash" and a rusty chipping treatment when finally in place.

Once the main components had been assembled I applied several layers of "mud" mixed from earth coloured oil paints and pigments. In the end I added remains of leaking or spilled fuel, grease and oil by the help of oil paints diluted with varying materials as mentioned earlier. Applying some wet effects evident in the original photo ended the weathering process.

uck 128kg
atü
u. Wabern

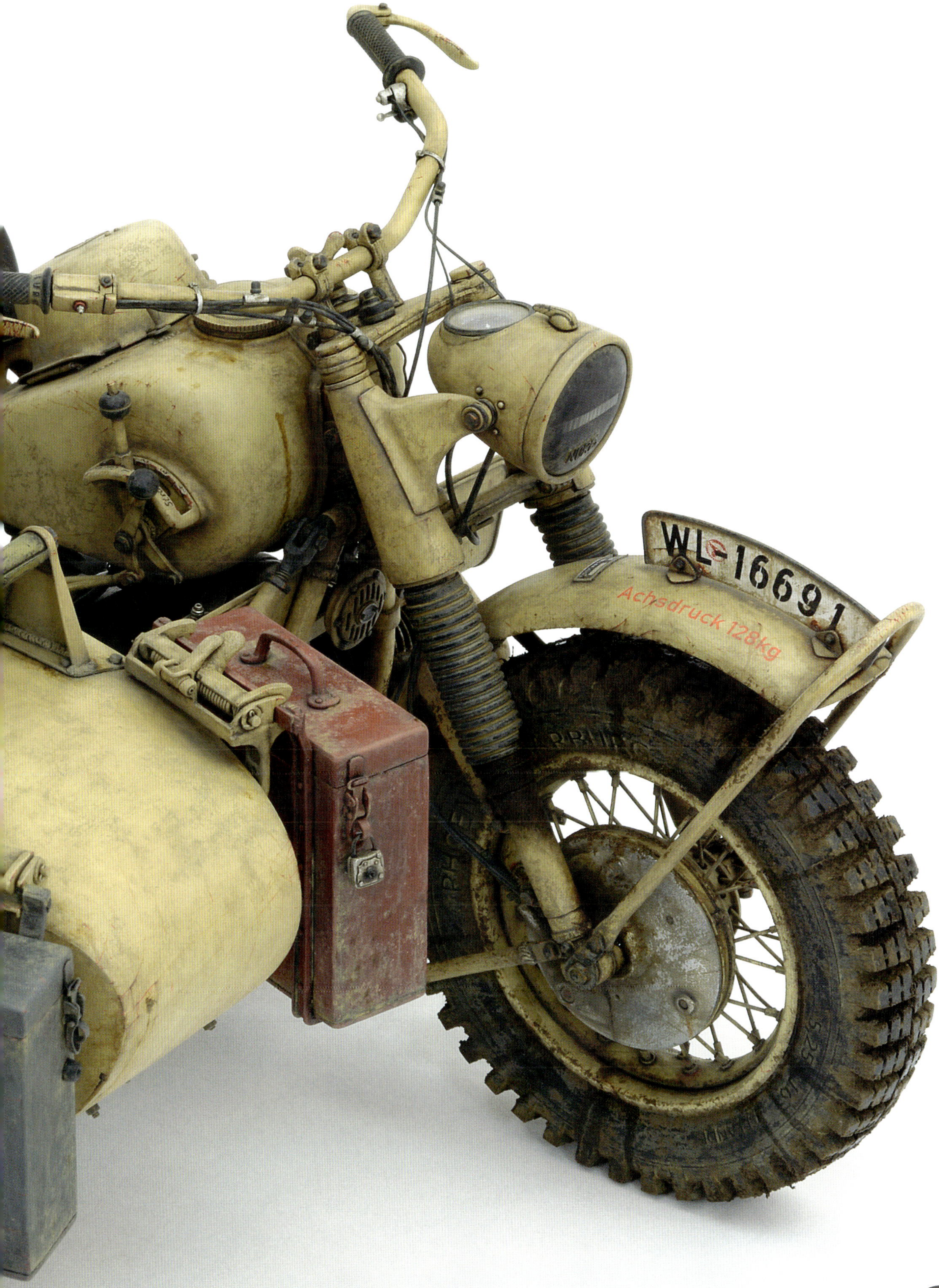
WL-16691
Achsdruck 128kg

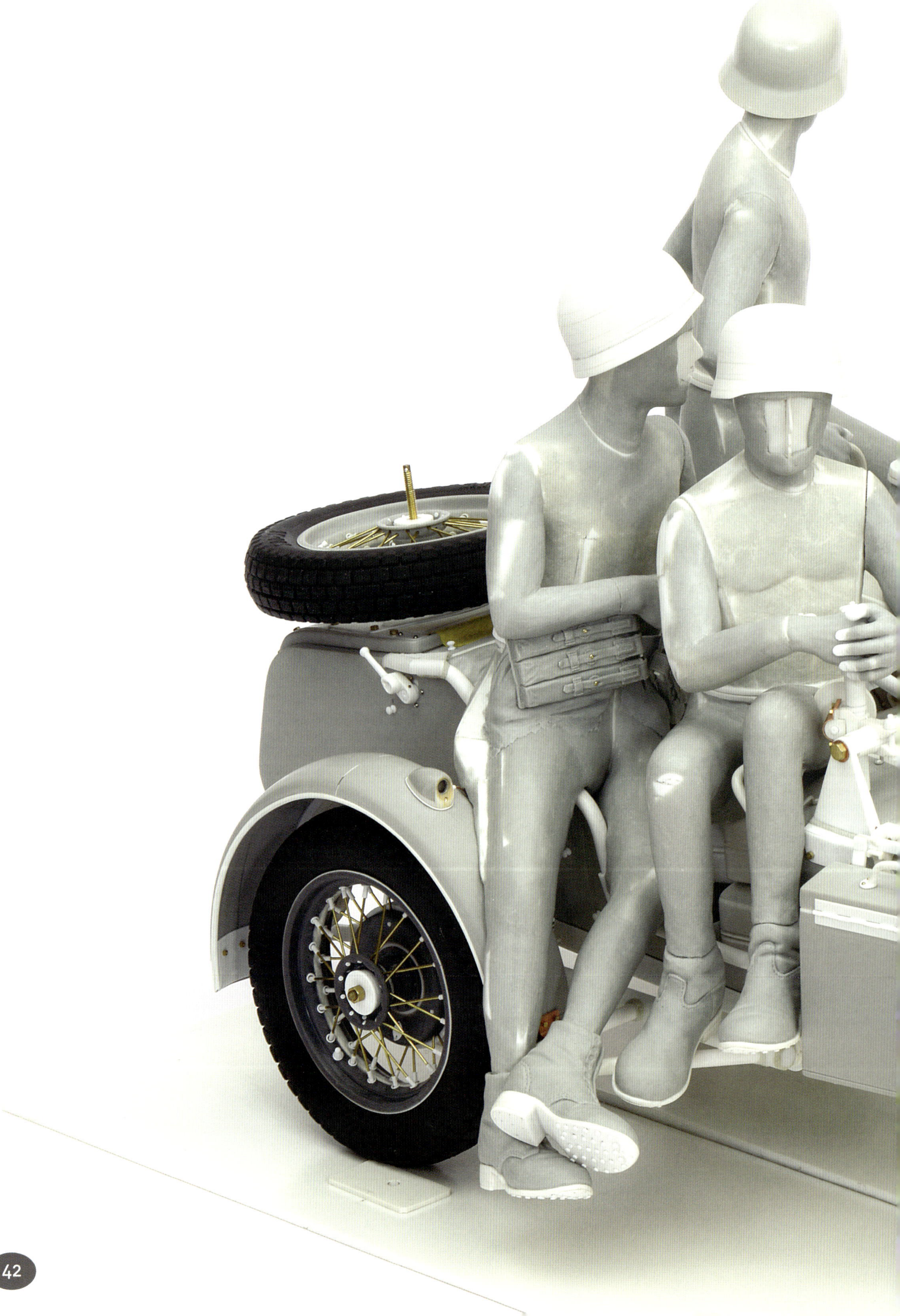

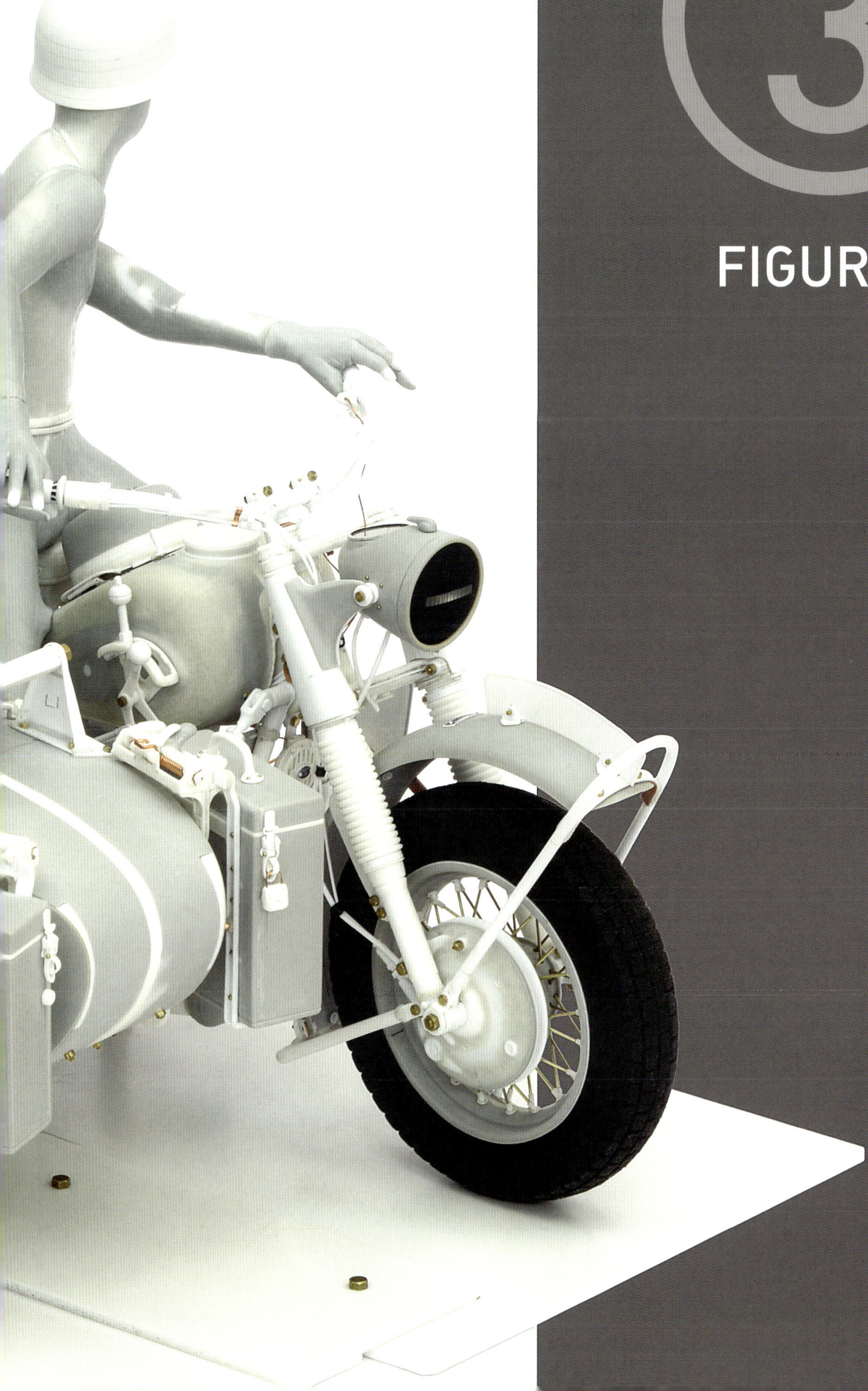

3

FIGURES

I have become familiar with sculpting my figures onto a kind of "skeleton" made of plastic parts which establishes the body proportions. This technique proved really helpful for adapting a group of four figures to each other on the one hand and to the model on the other.
I chose the soldier in the back of the sidecar as a starting point because his dimensions are rather clearly visible in the picture and it is also evident that he rests on the sidecar´s sidewall. Starting with flexible joints from copper wire the structure was stiffened with additional plastic tube sections.
Of course it is very hard to estimate the original size of the men in the photo but none of them seem to be extremely tall or small and so I chose an average size of 170cm to 175cm. Measuring my own body helped me to fix the right proportions too. In addition I checked the dimensions frequently with the original photo, which I had adapted approximately to the size of the scale BMW - in fact throughout the entire process of building and sculpting the figures I made regular checks.

The face's profile was cut from plastic card employing the scaled down original photo as a stencil.

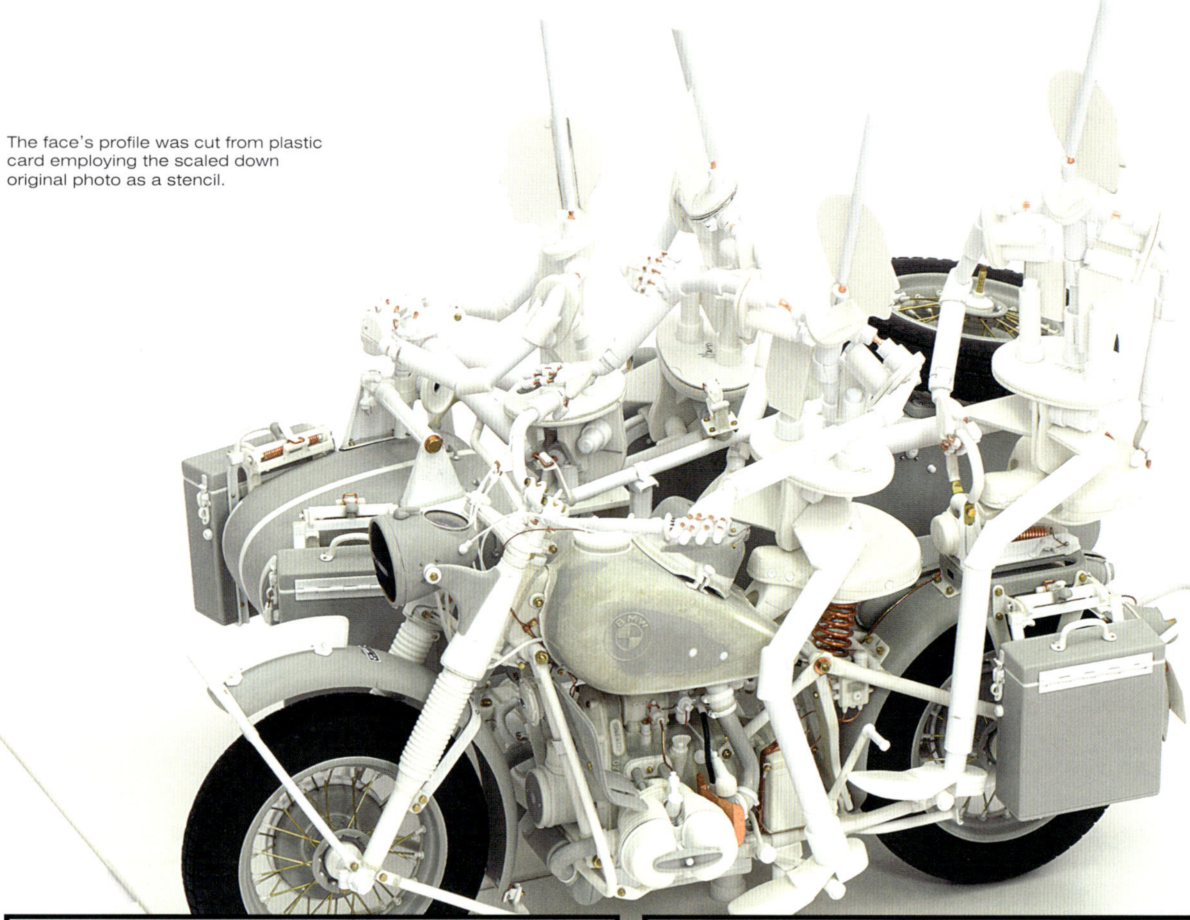

Head, upper body, lower body, arms, hands and feet were kept as separate units with rod/tubing sections providing a tight fit for test-fitting purposes.

The helmets were glued from several layers of laminated plastic card.

I made a hollow structure from plastic for all bodies to minimize the necessary amount of the heavy-weight Magic Sculp.

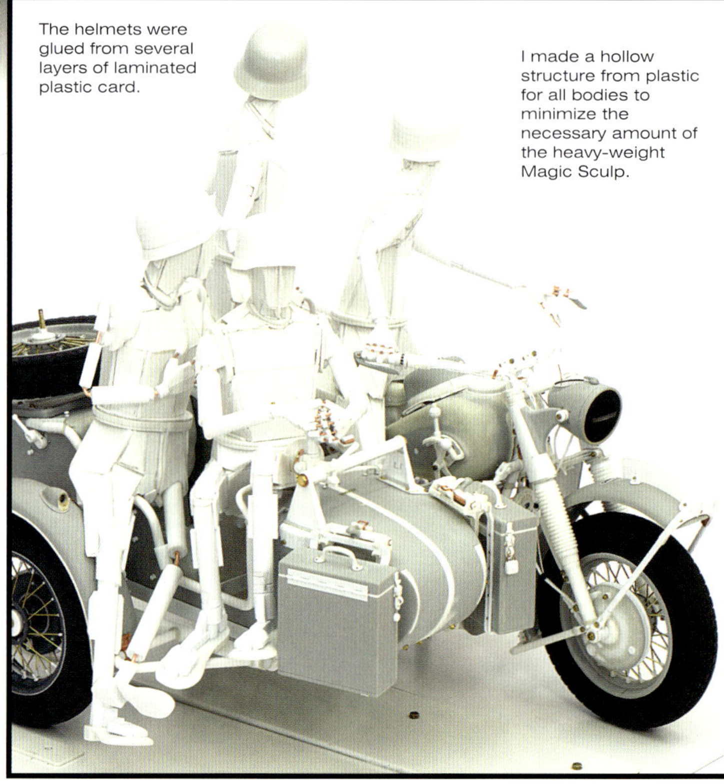

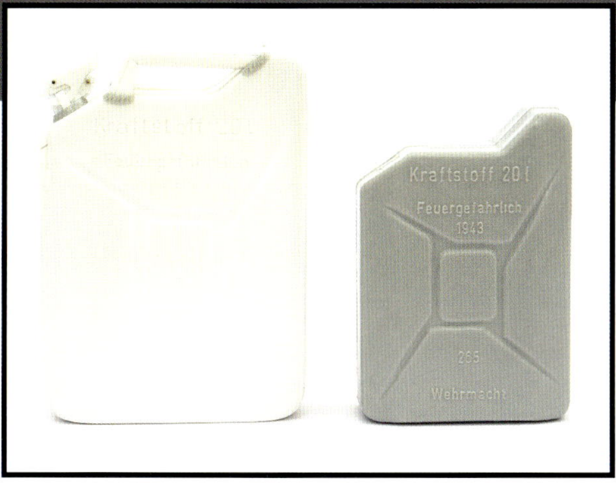

At first I had relied on the jerry can kit parts but I couldn't help notice later on that it was completely off-scale. Fortunately the depth proved closer to accuracy than length and width.

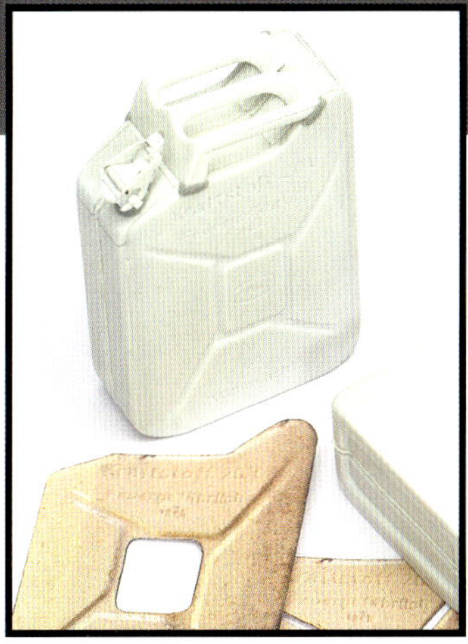

Scale copies of an original jerry can photograph were once more employed as stencils to allow scratch-building.

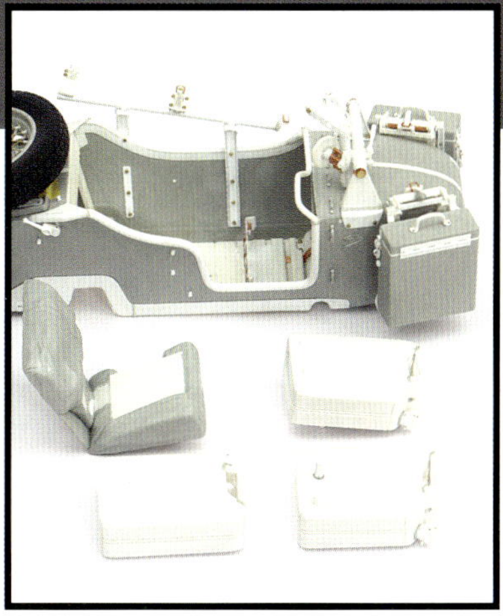

The three items were firmly fixed, but still removable, from the sidecar body and finally the new assembly replaced the first version of the seat.

SCULPTING THE FIGURES

The same procedure followed for every figure and I pushed the process forward step-by-step until the position of all of them was finally fixed with a first layer of Magic Sculp. The second figure sitting in the sidecar definitely rests on some extra equipment, which unfortunately is completely out of sight. I chose a total of three German fuel cans as fuel would have been important enough to be kept even while making the most hasty escape. As the kit parts proved heavily out of scale I had to make my own versions.

Afterwards I went on with the necessary steps to outfit all figures with a rough "naked" body including finished hands and boots in order to be able to finish each figure separately. I tried to make sure of a consistent quality level with all figures. That is why I chose to sculpt all four faces and heads first. I have picked out my favourite result (the driver figure) for the demonstration but all men were created not only equal but also in a very similar way.

The starting point was a rough version of the head's shape based on a stenciled silhouette cut from plastic card with a surrounding hollowed structure from plastic.

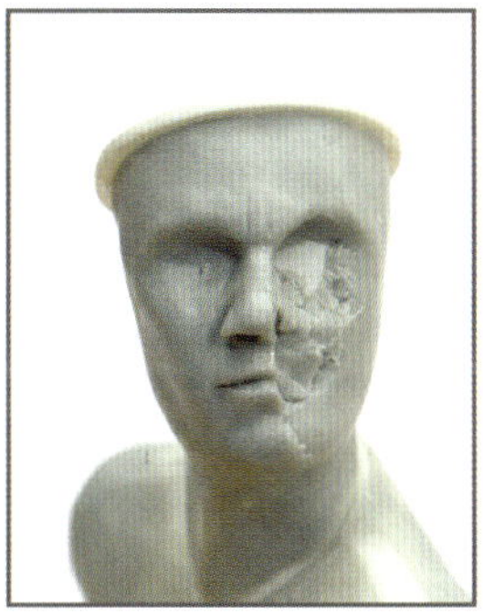

To split the sculpting process of nose, mouth and chin made it easier to keep the pre-shaped silhouette in the centre.

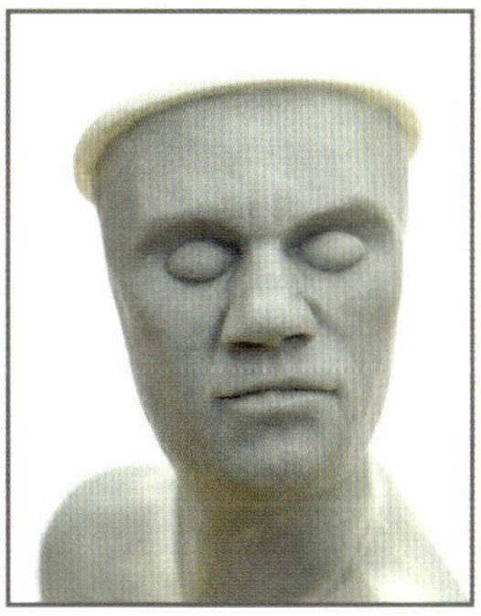

Pre-shaping the eye-balls simplified achieving symmetry and a smooth eye's surface at the same time. The latter would simplify the painting significantly.

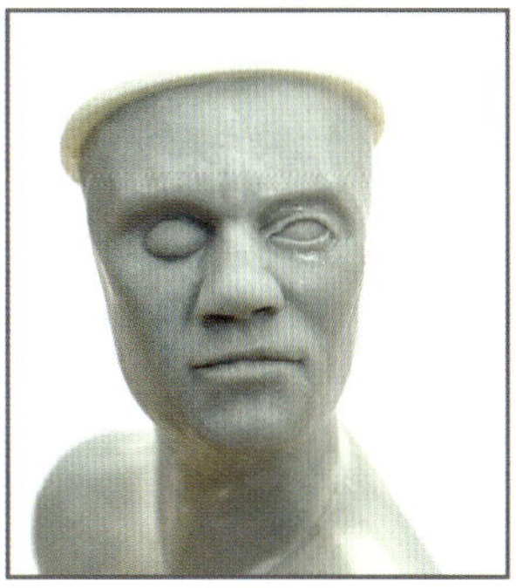

Making the eye-lids was split again. While processing the dried material was corrected whenever the necessity occurred. In this particular case the nose has received a makeover.

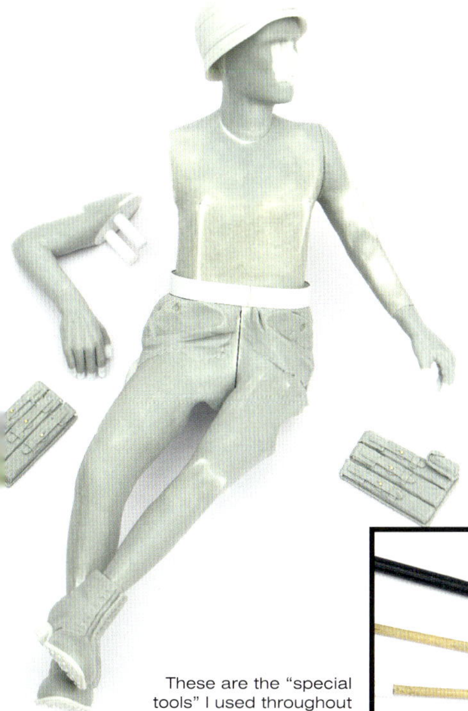

Finishing the rough versions of the naked bodies along with the hands and boots made me finally sure about the proportions. The bodies were kept thin enough to allow adding extra material but thick enough to avoid unrealistically deep folds.

As the right arm of the soldier in the back of the sidecar rests on the MP40 pouch both pouches were finished before the right hand could be. The lower left leg could be finally adapted to the finished right boot too.

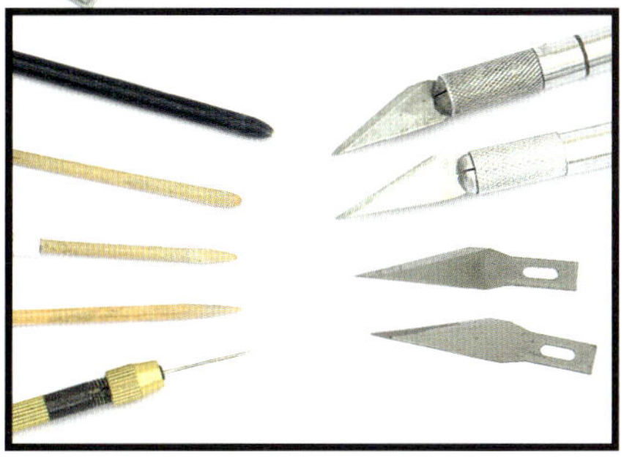

These are the "special tools" I used throughout the complete sculpting process. The blades sanded to differing curves were used to smoothen the dried material as well.

A fold in the upper eye lid was created by adding additional material.

Some more material gave the lower jaw a more defined appearance.

Creating the very complex shape of the ears is one of the most challenging aspects of face sculpting. The process was split again.

The basic lower hair line was added and structured with the sharp tip of a blade and a needle.

I added the helmet straps, in fact in several steps, with half-dried material rolled out on a flat surface covered with talcum powder. The clasp had been pre-produced from plastic material and copper wire.

The longer strands of hair were added after finishing the lower end of the helmet´s interior. It was simply structured with a blade while the putty was already half-dry.

The driver's helmet in the original photo most likely shows the strap of protective goggles which I sculpted in several steps using clear styrene for the glasses and sheet styrene for the framing - the latter pressed carefully into the still wet material.

Three of the helmets that are shown in the original photo seem to be roughly textured. Many German paratroopers tried to enhance the camouflage effect on their helmets and avoid shine by recolouring them by mixing paint with sand, sawdust or similar. I have mimicked this effect with a thin layer of Magic Sculp structured with coarse sandpaper.

The standard Wehrmacht infantry helmet, model 43, is a Revell kit-part from the spares box.

The soldier in the back of the sidecar is wearing a camouflage cover on his helmet, which seems to be not of the standard "Fallschirmjäger"-type but likely a tailor-made item.

After the interaction of the figures was established they were finished individually. For the documentation of uniform sculpting and adding equipment I have shown the chronological order and started with a detailed description of the first figure with only unique aspects (which differ from the first figure) of the remaining three are shown in more detail.

In the original photo the two soldiers in the sidecar are obviously wearing the German paratrooper's protective jump suits nicknamed "Knochensack" (bone sack) likely in varying patterns. Looking closely at the folding of the few visible areas of the pillion pasenger's uniform I decided he might wear the same. But the driver for sure shows a different kind of uniform, I was puzzled about this for quite a while. In the end a friend gave me the hint that this might be a coverall worn by Luftwaffe (air force) mechanics. I was aware that this was usually coloured off-white or black, which both is definitely not the case in the photo but I have found several items for sale on the internet coloured blue, which exactly showed every cut-detail visible in the photo. I finally decided to take this as the case. Once the figures were completed it was time to make at least a minimal base before the painting process could be approached.

The starting point differed from a "naked" version by the material fixing the pouches´ position and by the areas adapted to the sidecar sidewall and jerry can.

The upper body was made at first in several steps. The collar was made from sections of half-dried material leaving visible space underneath. Notice how the Y-straps are already prepared by indents in the uniform.

The back of the figure showing the straps realistically sat into the creases of the uniform.

Making the sleeves had already been prepared by sculpting the cuffs from half-dried material in order to keep the hands removable. The left sleeve had to be adapted to the MG42 transportation mount as well.

Making the trouser was the necessary next step, which of course made even more frequent test-fitting to the sidecar necessary.

My original plan was to split the figure at the belt line but I noticed that this plan would not allow me to keep the legs separated - in particular because of the extra equipment hanging from the belt. Thus I cut sections from the hip, glued them to the upper body underneath the belt-line and made the "Knochensack" ends from half-dried and rolled-out material applied to it.

The seams on the back of the water bottle show that it is of the larger version (1.0L instead of 0.8L) allowing the surplus refreshment of comrades (Labeflasche).

The last step to take was to add the buckle to the otherwise finished figure. I made a master-part from plastic material with details from Magic Sculp and cast it afterwards as I would predictably need three more of them.

While the "Luftwaffe" eagle-insignia was partly hidden by the Y-strap on the first figure it had to be completely sculpted for the second one.

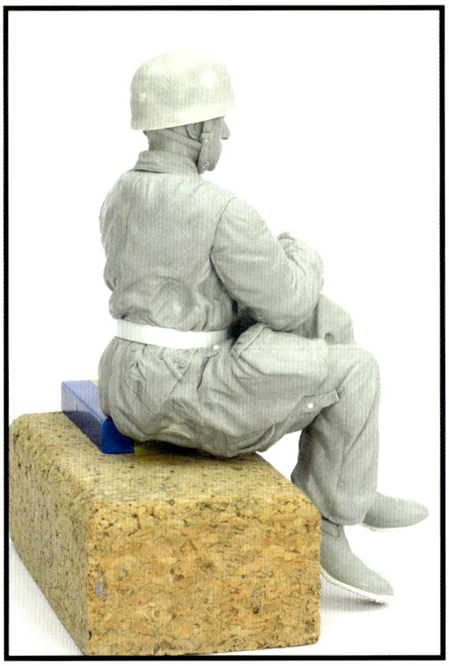

Sculpting the second figure followed basically the same path as for the first one but adapting him to the delicate MG34 mount, along with the hose pipe wrapped around it, providing an extra challenge. I kept the main screws of the mount loose and traversed the whole part forward to keep the figure's legs removable.

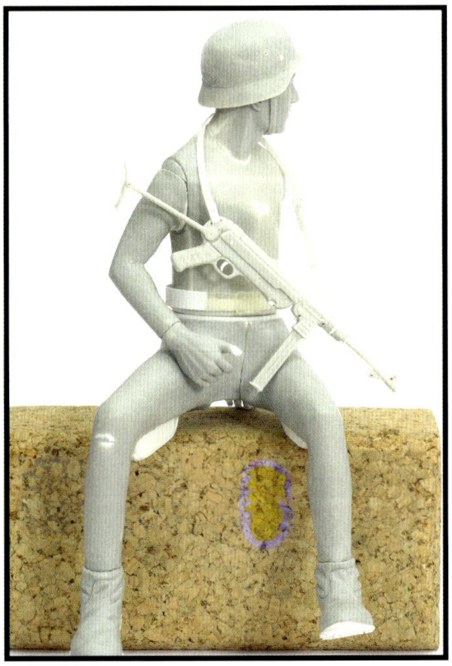

The pillion figure rests principally on the delicate plastic-made support of its seat. Only the right foot really provides extra support via the firmly fixed foot rest on top of the differential.

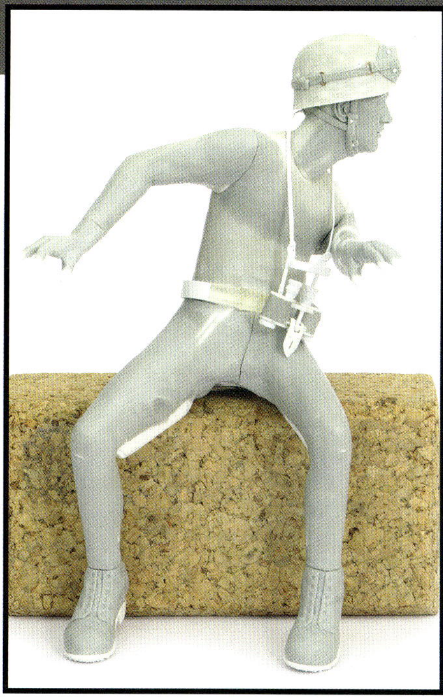

The oversize lower end of the coverall had to be adapted to several details of the motorcycle. While most of them stood the impact of half-dried Magic Sculp I had to fake the effect of the delicate shifting linkage with plastic tubing (seen on the inside of the right calf), which was hidden underneath extra material afterwards.

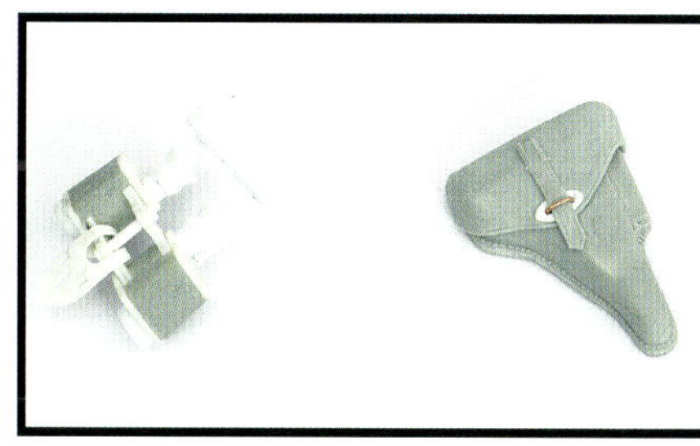

The driver clearly shows standard German field glasses hanging from his neck, which I constructed from plastic parts and made the central joint movable. The structured body was mimicked with Magic Sculp instead. I decided to add the holster of a P38 pistol also. Both items had to be finished beforehand and were pressed into the still wet sculpting material later on. I kept the strap of the field glasses a little lengthy and cut it afterwards hiding the split ends underneath the collar.

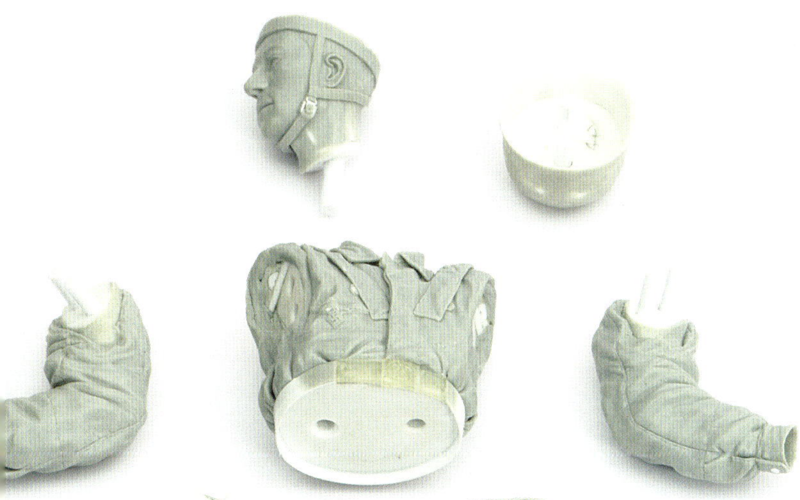

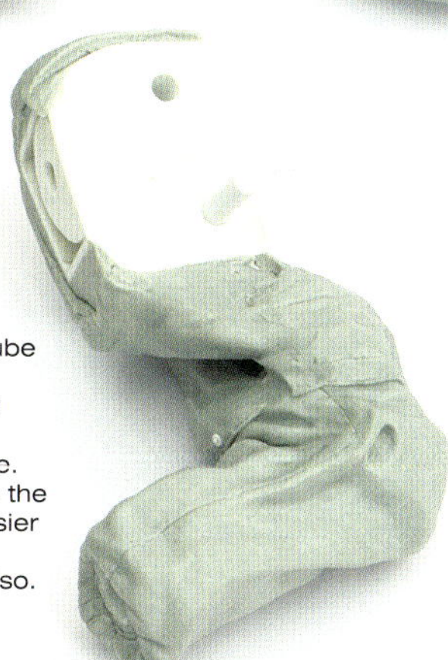

Working with rod/tube connections for all main parts made it possible to keep everything separate. This not only made the sculpting much easier but the following painting process also.

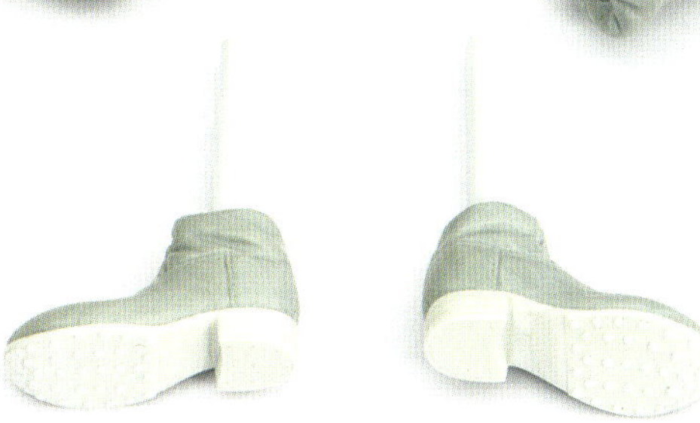

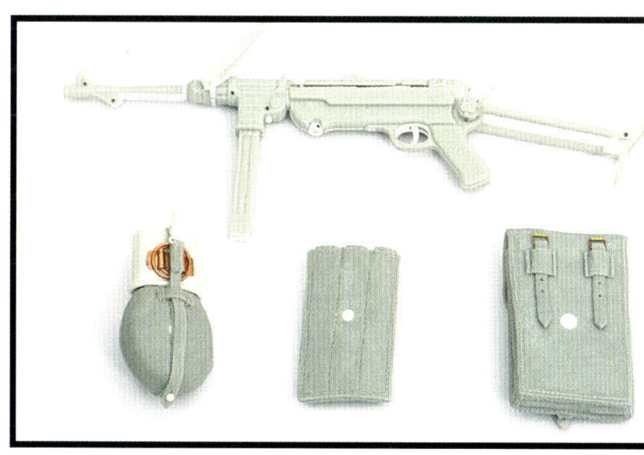
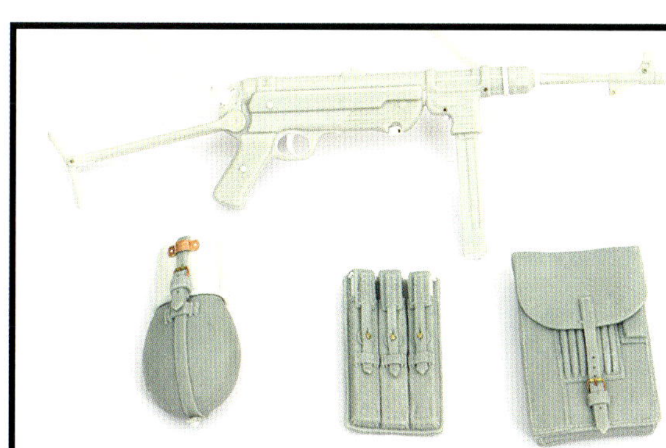

The extra equipment for the fourth figure was also pre-produced. The MP40 is a Revell item from the spares box with some extra details.

The strap of the MP40 was kept lengthy again and cut afterwards with the ends hidden underneath the collar.

I added grease to the plastic parts to keep the Magic Sculp from sticking to it while frequent test-fitting. Adding acid-free grease was my common practice whenever I wanted to keep the Magic Sculp from sticking to adapted parts but it does not work with the heavy tackiness of the freshly mixed material.

To sculpt the protective hand cuffs was rather challenging as these had to be kept divisible in order to remove the figure for painting. I started with the upper halves. Again, I made use of half-dried material rolled out with talcum powder and added grease to the finished parts. The pretty rough first result needed an additional makeover.The driver figure rests on the tank, which solved the weight problem comparably well.

4

FIGURE PAINTING

The entire figure painting was done with oils applied onto a semi-satin base of Tamiya acrylics.
Similar to the BMW model I fixed all separated figure parts to home-made handles to avoid touching them during the painting process which is even more important when working with the slow drying oil paints. As I did not glue the sub-assemblies to their handles but only jammed their rod fixings to tube sections they could be provisionally put together whenever necessary to adapt the shading, therefore I could avoid close to any corrections after final assembly.

Head-Painting
After all this scratch-building, sculpting and painting of the BMW model I felt I had run out of painting practice a little. Thus I started with painting some minor equipment parts and went then over to all four heads and hands. Again the documentation here is based on my favourite result - the driver figure.

The painting of all faces started with the details of the eyes in several steps. As I was after an atmosphere of tension I painted the irises only slightly touching the upper lid to give them a subtle staring appearance.

After mixing all necessary shades I started with painting the details of the eye-lids and the shadows around the eye sockets. Once dry, the remaining areas of the face were shadowed completely wet-on-wet in order to vary the colour shades by partly mixing them while applying. The starting point was the darkest shadow and the painting went over via the increasingly lighter shades to the details of lips and beard stubble. After drying the hair was painted as the last step along with the eye brows and after painting the helmet-straps everything was matted down with Model Master "Flat Clear".

Uniform-Painting
Uniform painting started with the driver figure wearing a unique coloured bluish coverall. The basic colour was mixed from Cobalt Blue, Sky Blue, Mars Black and Titanium White. It was varied with two darker shadow tones and two enlightened versions. To approximately match the pre-applied shade, the lighter shadow variation should be adapted to it instead of the base tone. The extremely large surface had to be painted in several sessions. To keep the necessary colour-mixes from drying the basic palette was immediately stowed in the refrigerator and only the small portions of paint necessary for each session were partitioned off.

As mentioned before, I had decided to outfit all three remaining figures with the typical German "Knochensack" jumpsuit. Though not clearly visible in the photo the example of the soldier in the front of the sidecar seems to be of the standard "Luftwaffe" splinter pattern while the example of the soldier behind does not show sharp edges of the camo pattern. I decided to paint the latter in the 1943 "Sumpftarn" (marsh-camo) pattern instead.
It is most unlikely that the pillion soldier would wear a unique coloured early "Knochensack" instead so I used this second figure to paint for a first test run of the "Luftwaffe" splinter pattern. In particular the numerous green stripes representing rain marks caused me some headache, keeping in mind that two more were to follow.
I had to make the figure in the back of the sidecar as the third because it had to be put in place before the figure in the front could be added. Basically I followed the same path as with the second one but with the additional challenge to create the translucent edges of all the camouflage dots.

Actually working on the camouflage pattern of three large scale figures stretched my stamina. Maybe this is the reason why I only fully documented the progress and painting techniques on the last figure when I could already see the end on the horizon.
The basic techniques were just the same with all three figures wearing a camouflage patterned jumpsuit - did I already quote that all men were created equal(ly)?!

The most adventurous aspect of finishing the last figure was to fit it in front of his already firmly glued comrade.

All eyes were coloured individually mixing one dark brown (Italian Earth/Brown Ochre/Warm Sepia Extra), one green (Verona Green Earth/Viridian) and two varying shades of greyish blue (Sky Blue/Cobalt Blue Tone/Titanium White/Mars Black).

The lighter shadow was mixed from Natural Burnt Sienna, Cadmium Red Deep, Naples Yellow Light and Titanium White. The darker shadow was achieved by adding Mars Black to this mixture and the basic skin tones by adding more Titanium White and Naples Yellow Light. Cobalt Blue and more Cadmium Red Deep were added to the shades for painting the lips and Burnt Umber provided the base for the hair lightened with Naples Yellow Light. The colour blobs on the right show the differing shades for the different faces. I did not mix them all at once of course but kept portions of every shade in the end in the refrigerator for eventually necessary retouching.

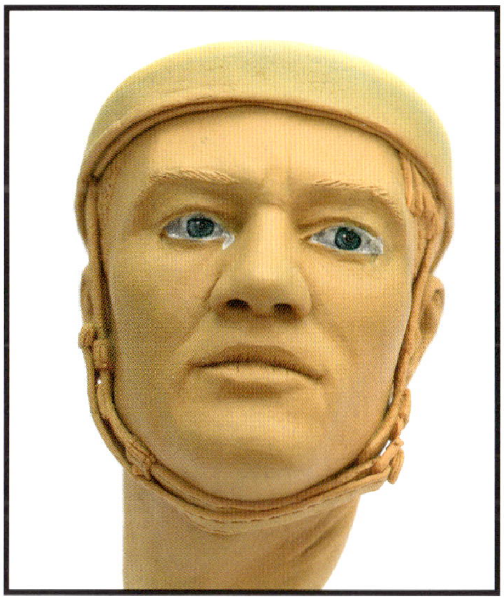

As already mentioned the irises were oil applied. The lighter areas were achieved by partly removing the oil paint with an additional clean brush. Only in the lower areas very small portions of white were added. This technique worked out best with bluish shades.

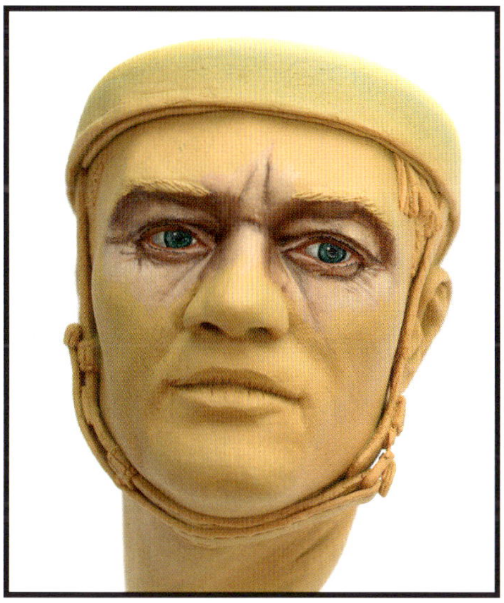

Shadowing the eye sockets along with the detail of the eye lids eased the following face painting significantly. I did not use the lighter, reddish shade in this area.

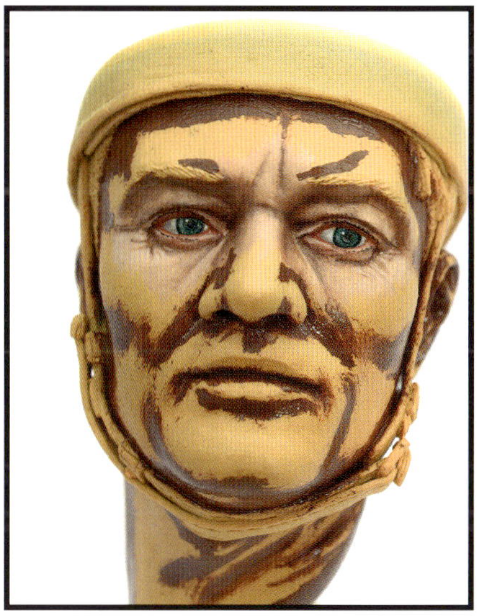

The dark shadow is far from reddish though it was created from the lighter one.

The reddish light shadow was only added to certain areas leaving the eye sockets, throat and lower chin untouched.

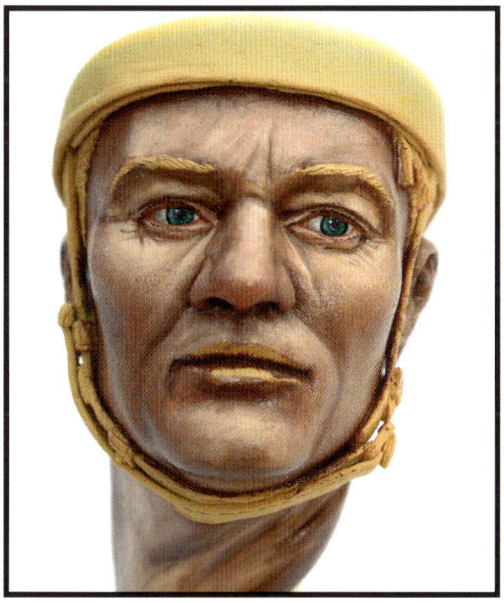

While application of the basic skin tone the shades were already partly mixed and blended to a convincing light/shadow-effect.

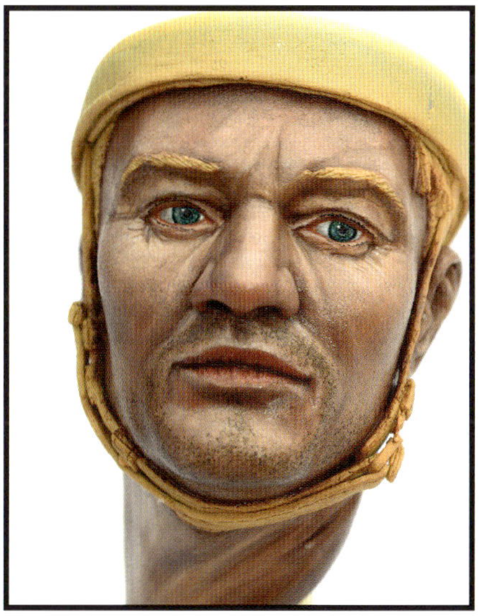

Along with further refinement and adding some highlights, the beard stubbles were dabbed onto the still wet base tones. I used Burnt Umber for the driver face, Raw Umber for a lighter variation (pillion and sidecar back figure) and Vandyke Brown for a darker one (sidecar front figure).

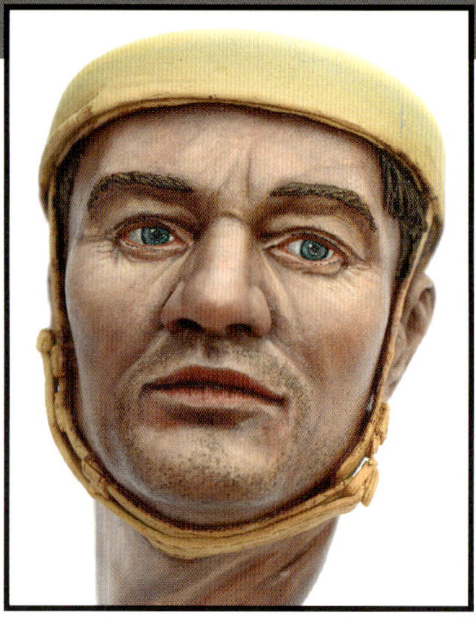

The finished result. Though hardly apparent in the photo the oils kept some shine after drying.

The matt varnish makes the colour transition appear even more subtle.

To put emphasis on the fact that the helmet cover was field made I painted it in "Heeres" (army) instead of "Luftwaffe" (air force) splinter pattern. Maybe it was made of a triangle tent section?!

All parts are fixed to handles. All parts apart from the coverall were already finished beforehand, which is not necessary of course but was helpful for rehearsal. The legs were not glued yet because they had to be fixed to the motorcycle separately.

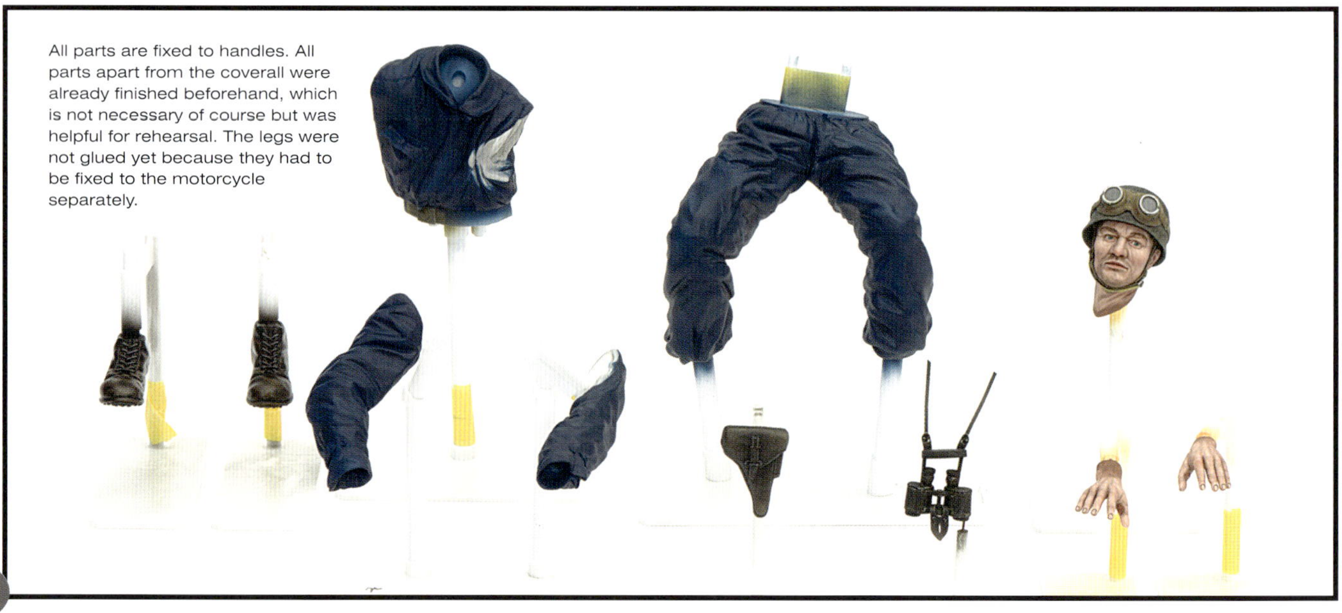

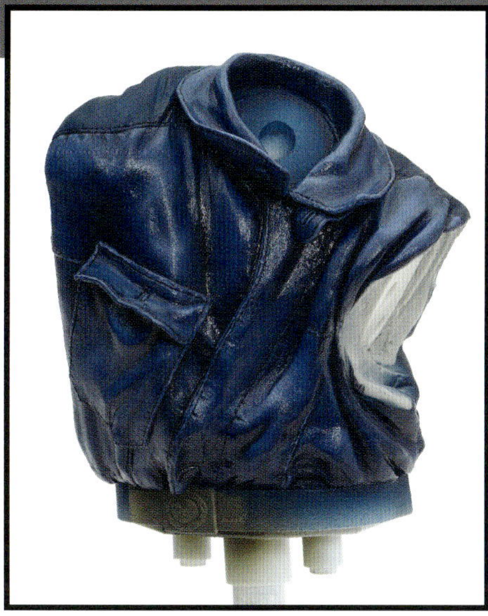

I started with the upper body´s front which made a handy portion to work on before I went over to the back, which I have chosen for the step-by-step process.

All shades were applied wet-on-wet starting with the deepest shadow going to the increasingly lighter shades. This technique allows you to create as many variations as necessary by partially mixing the different shades on the surface until the light/shadow-effect appears to be convincing.

In this case the basic acrylic colour shade seemed a bit dark to me so I corrected it while applicating the oils. The difference is apparent in this photo.

Finishing the shading on the entire figure was followed by adding some dirt and staining with varying oil mixes before everything was matted down with Model Master "Flat Clear".

The condition of the figure just before I fixed it to the motorcycle.

I had stayed skeptical until the end if I would manage to fix the hand cuffs after painting with a satisfying result. Thus I sculpted and painted the driver's hands with the same effort as all others. Fortunately it turned out to be unnecessary!

Basically the course of action was the same as with the first figure. I kept the legs split as well, because it was easier to paint the camouflage pattern in component state.

The camouflage pattern was applied with Revell enamels (unfortunately I cannot remember the exact mixtures) to the sprayed acrylic base tone. This provided the opportunity to immediately correct the edges with a clean brush moistened with white spirit. I relied on an original example shown in the images printed from the internet.

I painted the "rain marks" with oils instead (Verona Green Earth/Permanent Green Light/Mars Black/Titanium White) - again corrected with a clean brush moistened with white spirit whenever necessary.

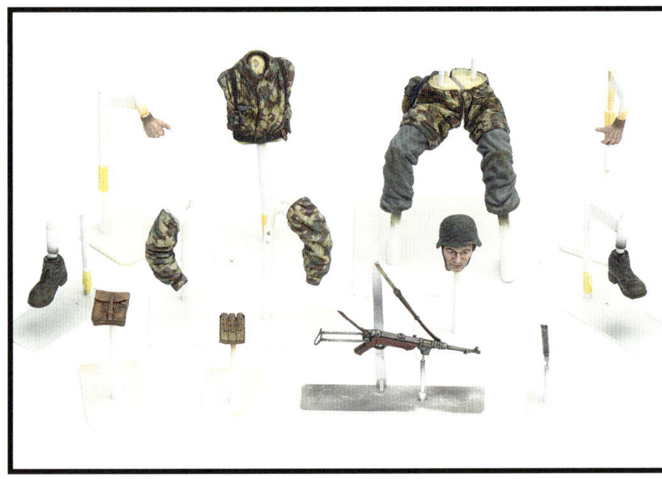

The parts are already completely finished and matted down. Notice the legs are still split.

These are the subassemblies just before fixing the figure. The boots were glued with PVA just before seating the figure, the left arm and right hand had to be fitted immediately afterwards.

The "Sumpftarn" pattern was originally developed from the "Splittertarn" pattern but the proportion of the green and brown patches were swapped. I started with the only sparingly applied brown shapes.

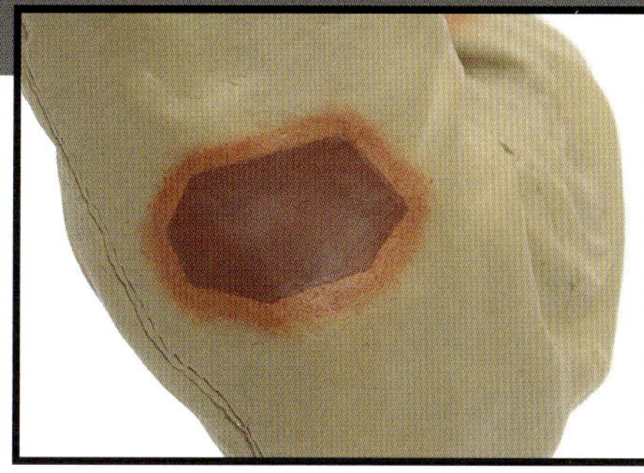

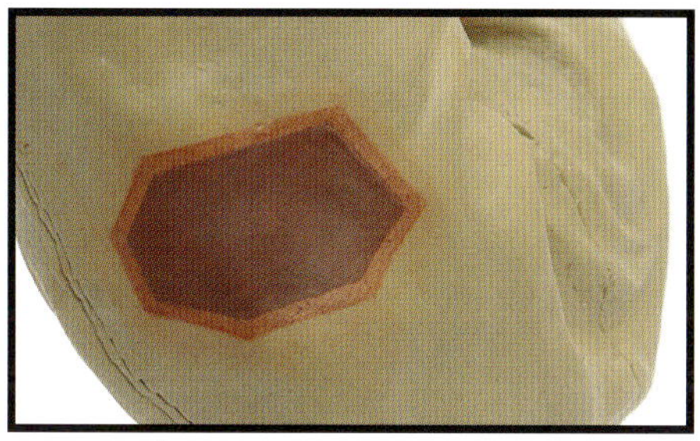

The translucent edges were applied with a mix of oils (Natural Burnt Umber/Naples Yellow Light/Cadmium Red Deep) in a "dry-brushing" mode and corrected with a clean brush moistened with white spirit afterwards.

The green areas were basically done in the same way - both again based on photos of an original "Knochensack".

The lines of the rain mark pattern were again applied with oils (Verona Green Earth/Permanent Green Light/Viridian/Italian Earth/Titanium White/Mars Black). The basic mixture was kept in the refrigerator and only small portions were used at a time.

All parts were kept separate until the end of the painting process. An extra challenge was the fact that the boots could not be kept separately and at the same time the legs had to be test-fitted several times to adapt the shading.

The figures not only hide some of the motorcycle details but parts of each other as well. This shot would have been no longer possible with the final assembled display.

This camouflage pattern was achieved again with Revell enamels applied onto a Tamiya acrylic base tone while taking another original uniform as a reference. The rain marks were oil applied again (Vandyke Brown/Verona Green Earth/Permanent Green Light/Titanium White). All colour shades were varied compared to the former examples in order to add interest.

Before I started shading the uniform, all details except for the national eagle were painted with Revell enamels and everything was sealed with semi-satin Tamiya acrylic varnish (X-22/X-21).

The shading started with outlining the details with the same "wash" I had used for the motorcycle, based on white-spirit-thinned oils (Vandyke Brown/Raw Umber).

Afterwards I added a translucent layer of 502 Abteilung "Buff" to the enlightened areas in a "drybrushing"-mode. But instead of touching only the raised areas with a wide brush I made use of small brushes working on the enlightened folds similarly to the usual figure painting technique.

Once the highlights had dried I did similar to the shaded areas again employing the basic shading Vandyke Brown/Raw Umber oil mixture. The effect can be varied with differing small brushes and simply be corrected with a clean brush moistened with white spirit as well.
After the shading was done I painted the details of the national insignia and the worn black belt with oils.

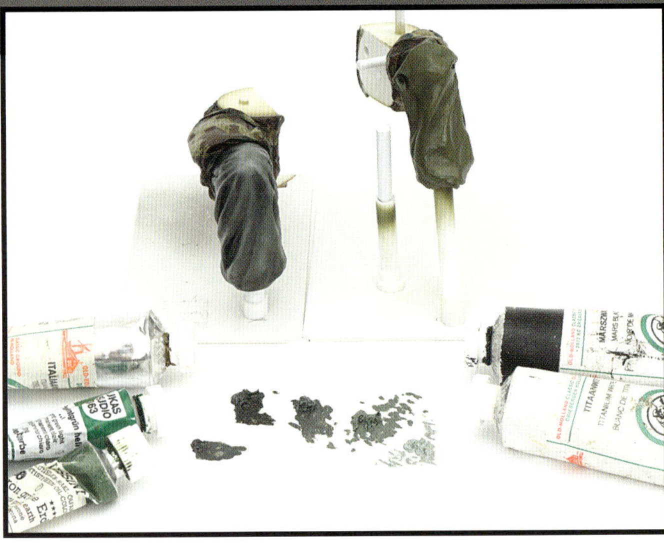

The Field-Grey trousers were painted with the same technique I had employed for the driver´s bluish coverall before. The basic tone was created by mixing Verona Green Earth, Permanent Green Light, Italian Earth, Mars Black and Titanium White. Notice the significant difference between acrylic base on the left leg and the final result on the right one.

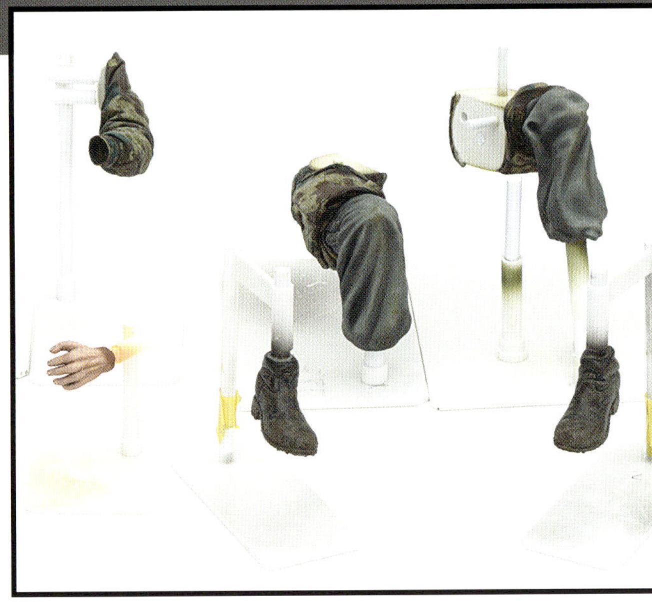

Extensive spills of grease, oil and dirt (again oil-paint based) were applied before everything was matted-down with Model Master "Flat Clear".

The glued legs had to be placed at first followed by the upper body with an already glued right arm - but without the hand. Afterwards the remaining parts could be added. I preferred to do so with the sidecar body apart from the delicate frame but everything had to be put in place with the PVA glue joints still manipulable in order to provide tight fit to the sidecar frame as well.

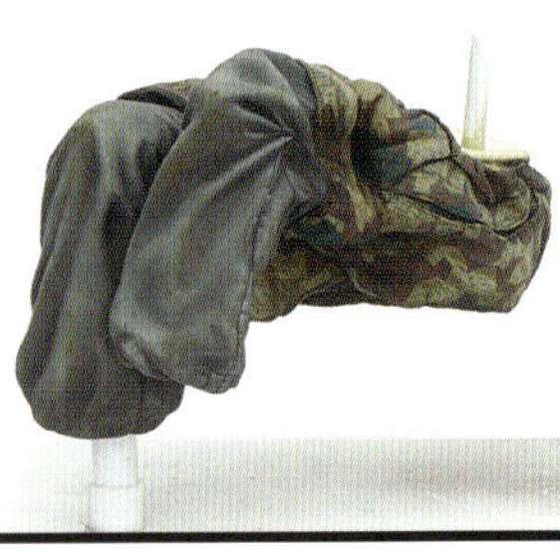

5

BASE

It had already been my initial plan to put the finished model onto a circular base with a protective glass hood and make it rotate electrically for exhibition purposes to put emphasis on the fact that it should be looked at from every angle.
Though I kept the model base as minimal as possible my plan made a pretty big and exactly made wooden base vital which was specifically produced by a professional wood turner.
Once the position of the model had been fixed it was possible to work only on the traversable inner section.

The model had to be placed onto the base very exactly as the glass hood fits pretty tightly. After that the tire's positions were marked and drilled in order to fix the model with threated rods and nuts in the end.

The gutter channel noticeable in the original photo was made of Magic Sculp applied to plastic sections of varying thickness. The thin outer rim of the base was carefully adapted to fit the irregular terrain about to be added.

Before proceeding with the groundwork I sealed the wooden base with semi-satin clear varnish (parquet sealant).

The gutter stones had been structured by the help of the tooling on the right. Varying shades of grey Revell enamels were applied in a heavily thinned condition in order to add variation.

The seams were filled with brush-applied Moltofill (household filler) cleaning the stones with a wetted cloth.

In order to keep the layers thin, the groundwork was prepared with a first smoothened layer of Moltofill.

For the final layer I mixed Moltofill with a fair amount of dark brown pigments and slowed down the drying process with some concentrated lemon juice. Onto the still wet mixture I applied some thinned pva and sprinkled natural sand and small stones onto it before I added imprints of tires and boots.

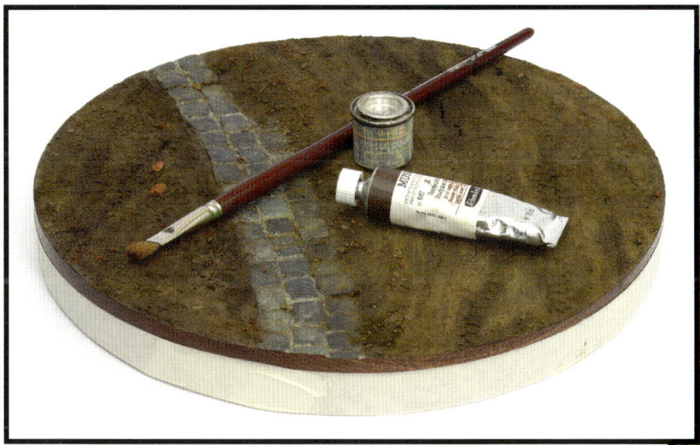

The result was toned down with a mixture of Revell clear and Vandyke Brown oil paint to achieve the partially wet appearance of the original photo.

Tonal variation was added with varying mixtures of brown pigments (Mig-Production "Europe Dust"/Umbra) and oils (502 Abteilung "Light Mud", Burnt Umber, Italian Earth, Naples Yellow Light) and some more of the shiny tone-down mixture of the preceding step. Tamiya "Clear" (X-22) was added to a few recesses as well.

„Besser schlecht gefahren - als gut gelaufen!"

German „Fallschirmjäger" of an unknown unit escaping from Falaise Pocket on a BMW R75. Bourgtheroulde, August 18th 1944

The finished base awaiting the painted model. The inner section rests on the internally fixed turntable. It will be finally fixcd as late as the BMW is in place as the model was to be nut-secured from underneath the wooden plate.

I have named the scene "Besser schlecht gefahren - als gut gelaufen!" meaning "better poorly driven than walked well!", which seems to have been a common phrase of German soldiers - while retreating in particular. The position of the two guys in the sidecar was presumably not really comfortable...

6

WARTIME

The picture that has made the basis for my model is of extraordinary high quality as it was taken by a professional "Kriegsberichterstatter" (war reporter) and obviously scanned from the original negative with the professional equipment of a national archive. This is a rare case as many others are privately taken and often the negatives are not available anymore with the paper versions being in poor condition - often extremely small compared to today's standards.

I decided to add some additional wartime pictures here though mostly of low quality. These may help expand on some more detail of the BMW R75 and the project I have described in this book.
At the same time they may serve for inspiration - or even make the base for you to take the challenge to completely rebuild one of them?!

In the 1940s heavy motorcycles were obviously still an attraction, therefore many privately taken photos show soldiers making memorable pictures with such a unique machine - unfortunately often of poor quality. The photos were likely taken in the winter 1942/43 on the eastern front. The soldiers posing along with the driver wear Field-Grey "Sturmartillerie" (assault artillery) uniforms. The BMW R75 is of late 1942 production type: It has early sheet metal front fork covers, the late style front fender and air-filter cover but still aluminum rocker covers and knee-shields but no protective guard for the left cylinder. Notice that the inner stowage box is missing along with its mount. A wire cable is fitted to the towing hook and wound around the outer stowage box mount (Th. Anderson Collection).

This BMW R75 belonged to the "Sturmgeschützabteilung" (assault gun unit) 191. It is of early production type. The fuel tank version showing rubber knee pads, a screwed coloured BMW-emblem and a late type, higher tank tool box proofs that it was produced between late 1941 and late 1942 (second version). But the front fender seems to be of the very early type with an extension on the right side, which was only produced until December 1941. Notice the early type leather stowage cases. The rear fenders back end is missing along with the stowage case, the rear support and most likely the pillion seat as well (Th. Anderson Collection).

Another BMW R75 of the "Sturmgeschützabteilung" (assault gun unit) 191 is used as a seemingly comfortable rest room. The fuel tank is of the same version as the one in the preceding picture. The front fender is of the early type as well but no longer outfitted with a right side extension. The front support is missing as are both sidecar stowage boxes. Notice the damaged position light and the bent fender. The spare wheel is not outfitted with a tire. This was a common practice even with new vehicles due to the shortcoming of rubber the Germans had to face (Th. Anderson Collection).

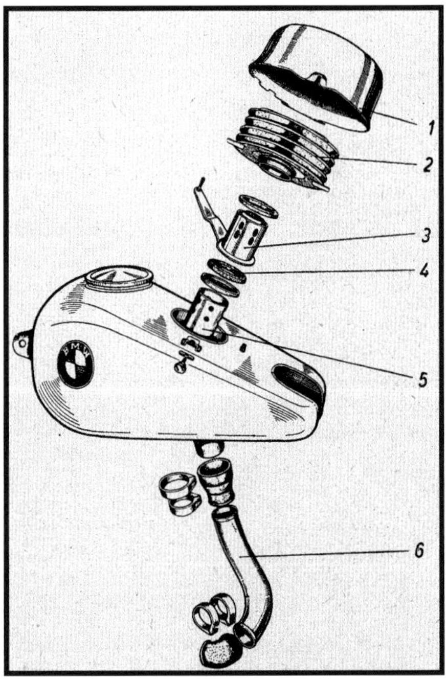

A schematic representation of the late type BMW air cleaning system was published in the "Deutsche Kraftfahrt" (German motor drive) journal (No.8/1943) of the NSKK ("Nationalsozialistisches Kraftfahrer Korps": NS motorist organization) for the interested motorcycle enthusiasts - and future soldiers (Th. Anderson Collection).

Left The late type front fender shows that this BMW R75 of an unknown unit must be late 1942 produced as other features are of more early type: The tank air cleaner cover along with a screwed coloured tank emblem (but dropped rubber protectors), the wider rear fender, the aluminum rocker covers and the sheet metal protective hoses on the front fork (Th. Anderson Collection).

Above The “Kradschützenabteilung” (motorcycle battalion) of the 24th. “Panzerdivision” (tank division) most likely on its way to Stalingrad in late summer of 1942. The motorcycles are still in just perfect condition. Actually only the emblems on the sidecar fender make sure that these are no Zündapp KS750s. Only the motorcycle second from left is outfitted with a MG34 mount. All show the early type leather stowage cases (Th. Anderson Collection).

Below Another BMW R75 of the 26th. “Panzerdivision”. Unfortunately the photo is of poor quality again and it gives little hint for the time of production except for the early type rear fender. But it is impressively showing the practice of heavy stowing. Notice the helmet clamped to the rear wheel support in particular. The sidecar fender had been obviously damaged and was roughly field-repaired afterwards (Th. Anderson Collection).

Left A BMW R75 obviously belonging to the 16th. "Panzerdivision". It is another example for heavy stowing - though all three original stowage cases seem to be missing. Likely only two soldiers manned the motorcycle at the time. It was a common practice to remove the early type fender in heavy weather conditions to keep collected mud from blocking the front wheel. Notice the fabric/leather night-drive lamp cover.
(Th. Anderson Collection).

Below An early-production BMW R75 of a "Luftwaffe" unit painted in dark grey. Unfortunately dog and driver seem to have been of higher interest for the photographer than the motorcycle. Nevertheless some interesting details are apparent. The BMW does show hardly any signs of use yet and it has not even received a license number. It is outfitted with the second tank version but the fender has no right side extension. There is no rubber tire on the spare wheel. (P. Spitzer Collection).

This BMW R75 of a "Wehrmacht" unit shows similar features as the preceding "Luftwaffe" example but it has a knee-shield, which in addition has a slot in the lower edge to adapt the September 1942-introduced heating system (but the heating system itself is not in place). Some minor damage at the back fender and sidecar body are apparent. The front fender is removed and the front tire is of non-standard type (P. Spitzer Collection).

Again an early-production BMW R75 of a "Wehrmacht"-unit in a close to perfect condition. It has the second variation of the fuel tank, no knee-shield or protective guard. Notice the unique non-standard headlight-cover for night-driving. The motorcycle is not outfitted with a spare wheel tire (P. Spitzer Collection).

BMW R75 of a "Wehrmacht" unit most likely in the winter 1943/44 on the eastern front. Like the featured scale model it shows protective hand cuffs for the driver but without the hot fume-ducts installed. The sidecar body heating system is in place instead proved by its adjustable muffler. The outer sheet metal stowage box is missing along with its mount. It seems that the vehicle has received an overall layer of winter-camo, which by now is heavily covered with mud (P. Spitzer Collection).

Another early-production BMW R75 of a "Wehrmacht" unit. The tactical marking shows that it belongs to an infantry signal platoon. Likely the driver is working on the valve-adjustment. Notice the rocker-covers lying on the ground. Though obviously in warm weather conditions a snow-chain is fixed to the spare wheel tire. Maybe for use in heavy mud instead. The sunken headlight cover suggests that the lens maybe broken. The sheet metal hoses on the front fork are of non-standard-type (P. Spitzer Collection).

Not a BMW R75 but an early production Zündapp KS 750 of an SS-unit most likely in the winter 1942/43. It shows three soldiers seated in driving position, which is close to identical to this on the BMW R75 due to the standard seats and sidecar body. Notice the common practice to keep the protective canvas covers for the opened sidecar body half fixed in order to keep it to hand. The position of the soldier in the sidecar seems rather comfortable though (Th. Anderson Collection).

Though unfortunately a bit out of focus the image interestingly shows the MG34 mount while in action. Notice that (differing from the main picture and scale model) it is mounted in an extreme right position and in front of the mounting shaft to adapt the gunner's size (Th. Anderson Collection).

Below This late production Zündapp KS750 shows the standard heating system in place including the ducts for the heated fumes to the hands and feet of the driver - in contrast to the model the hand cuffs are missing instead. Even though the vehicle seems to be in close to new condition the rear stowage box has already been replaced by an early production leather stowage case (Th. Anderson Collection).

Above A BMW R75 belonging to the 26th. "Panzerdivision". It was taken in Italy likely 1944. Both soldiers wear the first pattern "Panzer-Schutzanzug" (Panzer denim jacket). Only the driver has outfitted it with insignia. The motorcycle is of late 1943 production. It shows most late type features - just as the described scale model does. Notice the rubber protective covers on the front fork, the late type stowage box mounts and the sheet metal rocker covers in particular. A very rough camouflage pattern is vaguely visible (Th. Anderson Collection).

A very rare shot of a late production BMW R75 that has been transferred to private use as a solo machine after the war. It is repainted and the rear stowage box has been removed along with its support. The rear tire is of "Kübelwagen"-type the front tire is non-standard (P. Spitzer Collection).

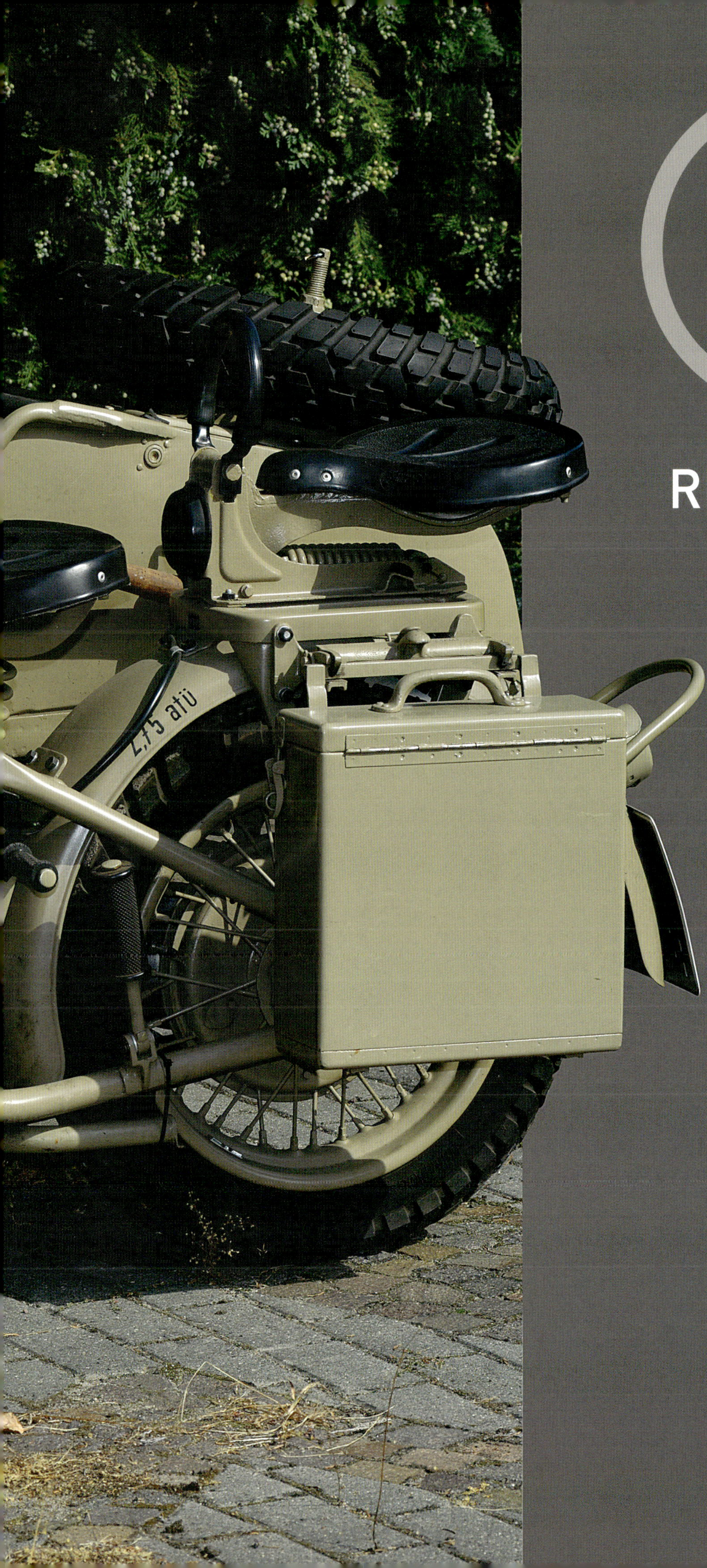

7

RESTORED

Restored vehicles usually do not exactly represent a historical vehicle of a specific production time but are often a mixture of differing types. Very few show matching serial numbers on frame, engine and sidecar frame like wartime vehicles usually did.
Many of them are still frequently driven and therefore show technical enhancements like modern type rubber tires or a rear-view mirror at least, which was never in use with wartime motorcycles.

Another basic problem is the fact that industrial standards for screw production have changed. In particular with wartime standards 8mm bolts used to have a 14mm head (instead of 13mm today) and 7mm bolts were in extensive use as well with a wrench-width of 11mm (which are completely dropped today). Very few restored vehicles really show original fasteners but modern, often silver galvanized ones instead.

As quoted before research on the internet will reveal a wide range of reference material, which in combination with the available literature on the BMW R75 - of H.P. Hommes in particular - provides a rather valid base for modelling.
Nevertheless a variety of photos which depict some rarely seen details maybe helpful and so I have added these as well.

The example shown has the serial number 750 160 at all main components, which means that it was originally of very early type as it was produced in August 1941 as only the 160th serial vehicle. It shows several late type characteristics though like the late type gas tank with an integrated air cleaning system and the late type mounts for the late type sheet metal stowage boxes.

The differential from the back side. The brake line is not placed correctly and the upper edge is broken. Notice the oil filler plug marked with red paint.

Above and below left The long holes in the flange of the rear sidecar frame tube allows adjustment of the internal torsion bar suspending the sidecar wheel.

Frontal view of the differential. Notice the union joint for the hydraulic sidecar brake in the bottom right. The late type right foot-rest for the pillion is mounted to the differential.

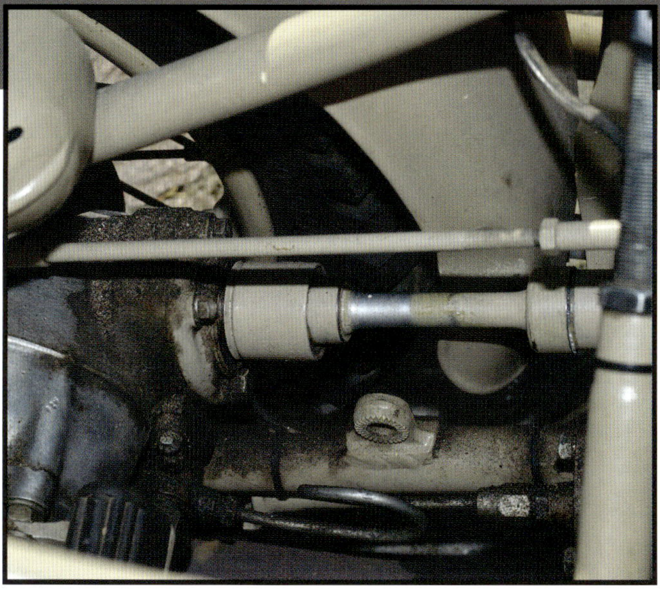

The inner sealing covers for the drive shaft are modern additions. Notice the early-type foot rest mount in the centre no longer in use.

Notice the difference between the wire-brush treated engine case and the glass bead blasted cylinder head and rocker covers. Unfortunately the "OZ74" marking is missing.

Left The early-production air cleaner housing was placed on the transmission. **Below** With the late type air cleaning system the transmission air vent once leading into the early type housing was protected by the small cover instead seen in the centre. Notice the resulting oil leakage.

Above The photo shows details of the rocker covers and left cylinder head. Notice the drilled fins reaching to the lower head screw.

Left The hydraulic rear- and sidecar-wheel brake reservoir is cast along with the rear transmission cover. The brake fluid filler plug in the center right is complexly shaped due to its vent-characteristics. The drive shaft is outfitted with a damper unit (center left) shown in a dark variant of "Dunkelgelb".

More details of the cylinder head's internal structure. Clearly visible are the upper of the four central head bolts showing a long hexagonal head, which is used as a base to fix the rockers.

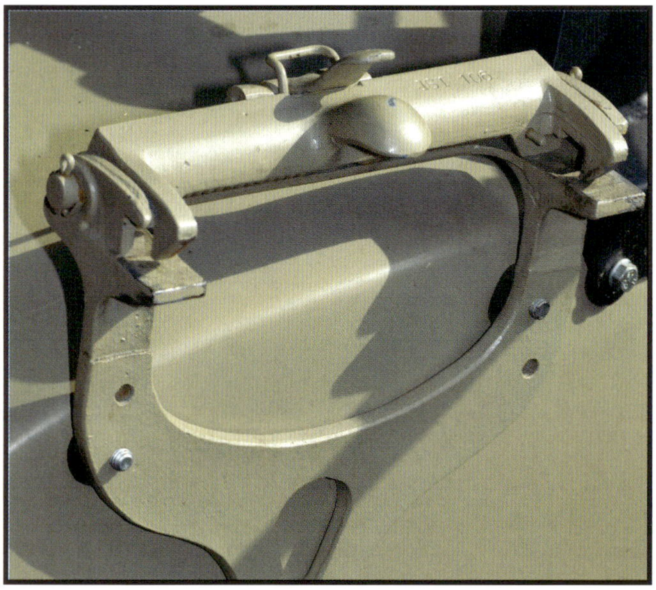

Details of the sidecar stowage box mounts. These were identical for both sides but used the upper threads for fixation. Notice the spring ends reaching through holes in the cast doubled hook-mount (only one is visible).

The inner mid spring-section was lengthened with the late-type mount and locked the additional securing tongue as well.

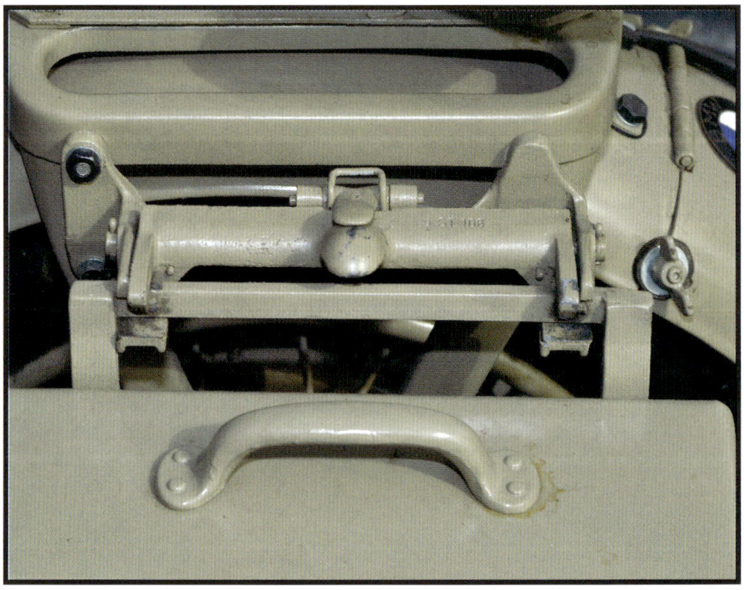

Above Details of the asymmetrical back stowage box mount.

Left The sides of the late-style stowage boxes are made of a single metal sheet overlapping at the back.

The asymmetrical rear fender support is adapted to the asymmetrical rear frame. It at the same time serves as a handle. The back end of the rear fender can be turned upwards in order to reach the rear wheel. The rear support is moved along that is why it's lower end is originally a butterfly nut fixed as is the fender's back end.

The small handle in the bottom right moves the internal lock fixing the pillion seat when it is not manned. The main handle is made of a rubber covered wire cable. Actually the triple-slotted saddle was only used on the early Zündapp KS750.

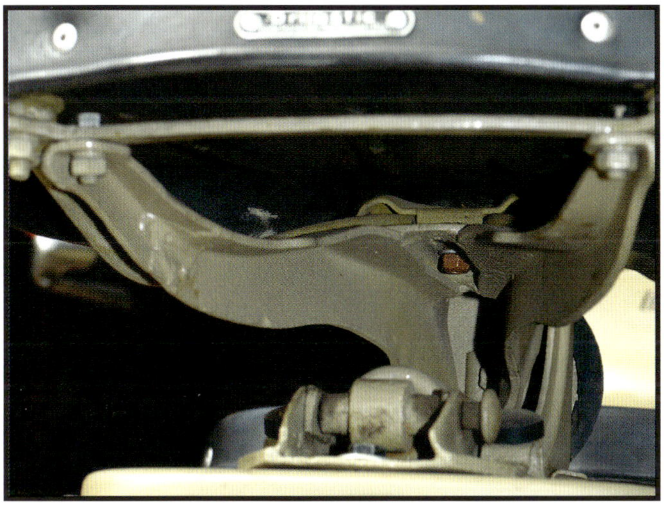

Details of the pillion seat support. Only the saddle pad along with the stretching spring supplied frame is identical with both seats.

The "Drilastic" material was a trademark of Dunlop, Hanau. It was widely used for German war time seats.

Details of the late-type tank including the integrated late-type air cleaning system and the hand shift levers. Usually the transmission is foot-shifted. But the hand-shift levers are important for shifting between street- and cross-country-drive and for choosing the reverse gear. For the latter the pin on the inner lever has to be pressed downward.

The underside of the fuel tank. The small frontal screw just connects both lower ends to each other with a spacer.

The back fuel tank mount is rubber supported. There seems to be a leak allowing fuel to run down the internal thread.

Above and above right The front fender is basically of the early production type but without the right side extension. The space between fender and tire is way too big - at least partly because of the smaller modern tire diameter. Notice that the right dip tube shows just the same leakage as the scale model (and its wartime paragon).

Right Details of the upper triple clamp with steering damper. In front of the handlebar clamp the kill switch is visible, which is connected to the magneto ignition system. This is the only way to stop the engine as the ignition is not battery-feed.

A special lock washer secures the butterfly nut-type adjusting screw for the steering damper.

Details of the steering damper unit underneath the steering head. The securing lower sheet metal tongue should be hooked over the pin in the foreground instead of being nut-fixed to the center.

The front mount of the sidecar frame allows adjustment to compensate tolerances in production. The central bolt clamps it to a spherical head at the end of the front engine mount. Originaly the screw was outfitted with a toggle, which was secured with a strap and buckle.

The towing hook was introduced in late 1942. The ring keeps a tow rope or cable from slipping off the hook.

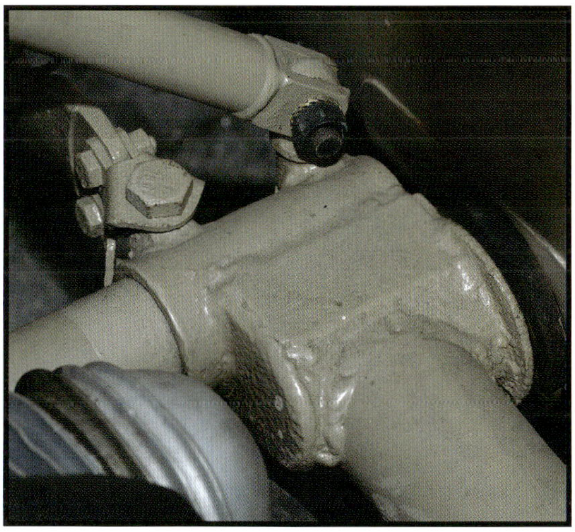

The tube clamp for the front mount is rather roughly welded to the sidecar frame strengthened by additional sheet metal sections.

Right Starting in early 1943 the left side leave spring mount was screw fixed instead of welded in order to allow adjustment.

Above With the late-style sidecar-drive all of it's sub-units were painted as they were no longer cast from aluminum but of steel instead due to short supply. Notice the oil filler plug is accurately marked with a red dot. The electric wiring for the back position light should be placed on the upper fender.

Left The clamp for the mid support of the sidecar frame is of late-type too. This means it's main eyelet is adjustable with a lock-nut-secured threat.

The rough sheet metal hinges support the delicate back of the sidecar body. Details of the central fender mount and the drive are just visible as well.

The locking mechanism for the sidecar back stowage space was connected to a shaft reaching through the sidecar body. The original key lock is missing.

The sidecar body was produced by several factories but "Steib" was the most common - and had the most appealing factory-logo. Notice the simple but effective fixation for the canvas cover.

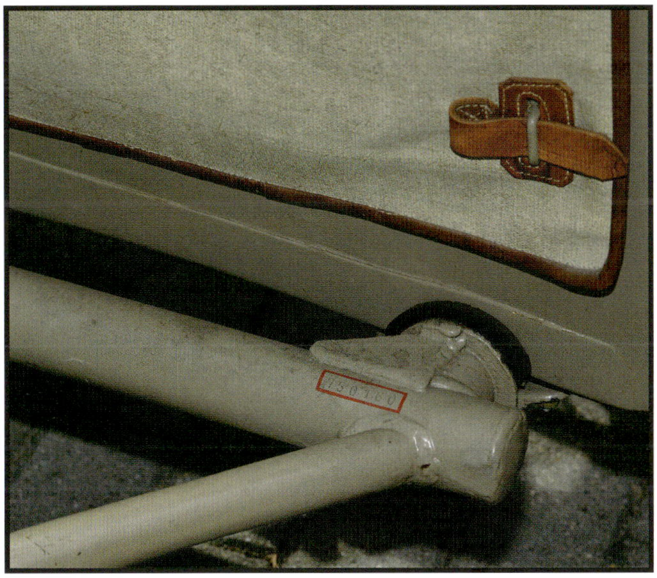

„Besser schlecht
- als gut

8

GALLERY

Mistakes have always been part of my modelling life - and I have always been frustrated by the fact.

Trying to rebuild a particular wartime photo meant an additional source of possible mistakes, which are at the same time more evident to others who may take the opportunity to compare the finished scale model to it's historical image.
I was aware of this effect and even willingly accepted some differences. For example I added a knee-shield, which the original picture does not show. I revealed this fact pretty late but did not want to miss this very typical late war BMW R75 feature.
In addition I am pretty sure that (though hardly visible) the historical photo shows the sidecar canvas cover fixed to the front mounts, maybe reaching over the driver's right leg. But I dropped this detail because it would have been virtually impossible to rebuild it in scale.

But of course there were other not willingly made mistakes also.

Thus rebuilding a particular wartime photo might be called an extra source of frustration. But on the other hand I am pretty sure that it somehow lifted my modelling up to a higher level of realism and historical correctness while it still left the necessary space for some artificial license in order to create a convincing looking scale model in the end. So rebuilding a historical photo was at the same time a source of inspiration and in the end satisfaction, too.
I can highly recommend this process of modelling whenever one keeps in mind that perfection will be out of reach with it - like with all other kinds of modelling!

1.75 atü
Reifen-Klotz Kassel u. Wabern

WL-16691

The oil leak at the upper dip tube was a frequent effect on BMW R75 front forks.

BMW

Notice the back stowage box sprayed in a variant of "Dunkelgelb" with a "Dunkelgrün" camouflage pattern suggesting that it was salvaged from another motorcycle. I did the same with the sidecar wheel but the effect is only vaguely visible under the "mud".

WL 16691
Achsdruck 128kg

Items used:

ABER: R-03, Z-P176
Archer: AR88007
Paper Panzer Productions: PPP 35017
Revell: 03070 (BMW R75)

Acknowledgements:

I am very grateful that with this project, model and book, I could rely on the support of several friends (in alphabetical order): Thomas Anderson, Falk Greiner, Frank Daugs, Waclaw Peszko, Jörg Schulz, Peter Spitzer and Thomas Warneke.

I want to dedicate this book to my beloved daughter, Johanna.

References:

David Doyle, German Motorcycles of WWII. A Visual History in Vintage Photos and Restored Examples, Part 1, no loc. 2016 (ISBN 978-1-944367-02-2)

Ersatzteilliste für das Kraftrad BMW R75 750ccm mit Seitenwagen (angetrieben), Ausgabe B, München 1942 (Reprint)

Hans-Peter Hommes, Bilderbuch BMW R75 + Zündapp KS 750, Jüchen 2004 (no ISBN)

Id., Detaillierte Beschreibung des Wehrmachtgespanns BMW R 75, Viersen/Jüchen 2009 (no ISBN)

Id., Das Wehrmachtsgespann BMW R75. Dokumente, Zeichnungen und Fotos; English/German Version, Jüchen 1999 (no ISBN)

Id., Peter's Werkstatthandbuch. Zündapp KS 750/BMW R75, Jüchen 2007 (no ISBN)

Frantisek Koran/Michal Burian, BMW R75 in detail. BMW R75 WWII Motorcycles with Sidecar from Vladimir Lehar Private Collection; Photo Manual for Modellers, Prague 2002 (ISBN 80-86416-17-8)

D 605/5: Schweres Kraftrad 750cm3 mit Seitenwagen (angetrieben) BMW Typ R75. Gerätebeschreibung und Dienstanweisung. Vom 27.6.41, Berlin 1941 (Reprint)

Jean Paul Pallud, Rückmarsch! The German retreat from Normandy; Then and Now, 2nd issue, Essex 2007 (ISBN 1-870067-57-6)

Roly Pickering, Ausrüstung Vol. 1. Field Equipment of the German Forces in World War II, 2nd ed., Hitchin 2015 (ISBN 978-1-62847-594-4)

Id., Ausrüstung Vol. 2. Field Equipment of the German Forces in World War II, 2nd ed., Hitchin 2015 (ISBN 978-1-63068-823-3)

Janusz Piekalkiewicz, Die BMW Kräder R12/R75 im Zweiten Weltkrieg, Stuttgart 1977 (ISBN 3-87943-446-8)

Karl Veltzé, Deutsche Fallschirmjäger. Uniformierung und Ausrüstung 1936-1945; Bd. 1: Bekleidung, Berlin 2015 (ISBN 978-3-938447-80-2)

id., Deutsche Fallschirmjäger. Uniformierung und Ausrüstung 1936-1945; Bd. 2: Helme, Ausrüstung und Bewaffnung, Berlin 2016 (ISBN 978-3-938447-81-9)

Id., Deutsche Fallschirmjäger. Uniformierung und Ausrüstung 1936-1945; Bd. 3: Abzeichen, Dokumente und Kampfeinsätze, Berlin 2018 (ISBN 978-3-938447-82-6).

Links:

www.fahrzeuge-der-wehrmacht.de
www.kuebelwagen.net
www.panzerbasics.com
www.pistor-modellbau.de
www.primeportal.net
www.tailormadedecals.com
www.tola-tools.de
www.wehrmachtsgespann.de
www.weitze.net